To Pearl — my
favorite story teller

Ernie

The Kid Was a Hustler

Ernest G. ZumBrunnen

iUniverse, Inc.
Bloomington

The Kid Was a Hustler

Copyright © 2010 Ernest G. ZumBrunnen

iUniverse books may be ordered through booksellers or by contacting:

iUniverse
1663 Liberty Drive
Bloomington, IN 47403
www.iuniverse.com
1-800-Authors (1-800-288-4677)

ISBN: 978-1-4502-7395-4 (pbk)
ISBN: 978-1-4502-7397-8 (cloth)
ISBN: 978-1-4502-7396-1 (ebk)

Printed in the United States of America

iUniverse rev. date: 11/18/2010

ACKNOWLEDGMENT

I appreciate the contributions to this book by Jean McKinney, Amy Hawes, Liz Crain, and John Hawes for their reading, proofing, and helpful suggestions, and to Grace Hawes for her editing.

TO OUR ADORABLE GRANDCHILDREN

Rebekah ZumBrunnen

Sarah ZumBrunnen

Joshua ZumBrunnen

Erik Hawes

Nicole ZumBrunnen

Roger Crain

Reza Mollaghaffari

Janelle ZumBrunnen

Max Crain

Mariam Mollaghaffari

Garrett ZumBrunnen

Carrie Hawes

Connor Progin

Contents

INTRODUCTION

My working life started in 1932, when I was six years old. The country was in the grip of The Great Depression. Practically nobody had any money. The unemployment rate was much higher (24.9%) than it is now in 2010 (9.5%). The major problem of each day in 1932 was finding enough money for the next meal.

As a six year old, I was not even remotely aware of that concern. My immediate problem was my need for bubble gum and marbles. So it was up to me to figure out how to earn the pennies to solve this problem, as well as similar ones that were to follow. Along the way, the lessons I learned would serve me well for my entire life.

The percentage of our current population, who lived through those terrifying years, is diminishing rapidly. Accordingly, this may well be one of the very last books that will be written about that era, and how one of us was able to survive it.

Hustle—To gain by energetic effort: The freedictionary.com

CHAPTER 1
THE YOUNG HUSTLER

Who knew? Looking back more than 80 years to my boyhood in Brooklyn, Wisconsin, I am easily convinced that we were very poor at the time. But so was almost everyone else. It's hard to tell the difference, when you are all in the same proverbial boat. But when times are good, it is quite easy to notice certain differences. Two of my grandchildren have on more than one occasion said to me: "Grandpa, you're rich, aren't you". And surely I am, when compared to some others they know.

But I believe they can see, just as I could at their age, that wealth does not assure happiness. One need not look too far to observe rich people who are miserable. I do not envy their possessions and I suspect they may have made ill use of their good fortune. They are what has led me to the conclusion: "It's what you do with what you've got that counts"!

The rather recent outpouring of personal wealth for the benefit of those in need is really quite heartwarming to all of us. Examples of philanthropists include Bill Gates, Oprah Winfrey, Warren Buffett, Paul Allen, Phil Knight, Ted Turner and Ken Behring. Their actions speak volumes. But so can yours and mine. Let us not forget the biblical story of the widow's mite, which valued the tiny gift of the poor widow over the much larger gift of the man who could easily afford it.

All of this pretty well sums up my present feelings. But in 1930, when I was four years old, things were a lot different. The country was in terrible financial condition. Nobody knew when it might end, or if it ever would. My uncle, Harry Baldwin and his wife Clara had taken me in as a two year old whose mother had just passed away. Uncle Harry had graduated from the University of Wisconsin in Madison, had been an instructor in agriculture at Texas A & M University for a short time, and then had decided to operate as an electrician. He owned a homemade airplane and flying it was his hobby. Aunt Clara had grown up on a farm and had been a teacher in a one-room schoolhouse. Sadly, uncle Harry crashed his plane and was killed when I was four years old. That left his widow with the awesome responsibility of being a "single parent", caring for me as well as for herself and my father, her brother.

I don't recall my father contributing very much to our livelihood at the time. I can only attribute this to his deep grief over my mother's death, but cannot excuse him on that basis. My recollection is that he didn't really return to a productive life until a number of years later when he met Margaret McNabb. She was a fifth grade schoolteacher who had grown up on a farm in northwest Wisconsin. Her wonderful influence on him was life changing. Incidentally, she and my dad waited until I was eighteen and my brother was twenty-one before they married, and then only after asking us if we thought it would be all right. We did!

Meanwhile, Aunt Clara supported us by working in the local post office, and by performing some part time work at the public library. My memory is that we were never hungry, although the fare would hardly make anyone's list of the ten best examples of outstanding nutritionally sound diets. We ate a lot of potatoes, macaroni and cabbage and had a vegetable garden every summer.

Carrots and squash were special treats and every now and then we had bologna. Being of 100% Swiss ancestry the consumption of cheese was mandated whenever the budget allowed.

The thing that was really almost non-existent was "spending-money". Aunt Clara often told me she would like to do things for me, but just could not afford them. I recall having shared her disappointment at the time! Later on in life, I came to understand how wonderful this lady had been to take me into her home, feed me, clothe me, teach and encourage me, and to raise me to manhood. My appreciation for all of that is profound.

Returning to the concept of "spending money", it is more than likely an important thought in the life of any young boy. I was no different. Perhaps if she had been able to pay it, I might have received an allowance, tied to the performance of necessary chores. As far as I knew, my dear friend Bryant Wackman, the banker's son, was the only kid in town who received an allowance and he was required to sweep the bank floor on a daily basis. I remember that I loved the smell of sweeping compound, which seemed to combine the aromas of rubbing alcohol and a stroll through a pine forest. The only two regular opportunities to inhale this delightful bouquet were to hang around Bryant at work, or to pester Tony Kroyer, the beloved janitor at our school.

The predicament of not having "spending money" was indeed a gloomy one. And so it was, that I believed it necessary to devise a plan. My earliest memory of such a plan was at age six, when I became something of a "hustler". I was somehow able to convince some of our neighbors that they needed their sidewalks swept in the spring, summer and fall, and shoveled free of snow during the winter. They also needed their lawns mowed for much of the year and raked free of leaves in the fall.

But there was not much money floating around. So you can imagine how important it was to hone one's salesmanship skills, in order for a six-year-old to get a poverty- stricken adult to part with some of these meager funds. I have often wondered what percentage of my success was attributable to sales skills, and what percentage was due to being a "cute little kid", who was a hard worker and needed some adult encouragement and support. More of the latter I suspect; however, the sales skills I developed have always been of substantial benefit to me.

Chuck Yarwood, a wiry, energetic young man lived across the street from us. Although he was three years older than I, he recognized that my hard work matched his own work ethic and that I would make a worthy "business partner". Chuck had some great ideas and the newly formed partnership was destined to make some really serious money, right up to the day of Chuck's high school graduation.

This relationship also provided some other fine perks. Chuck had a single-shot 410-gauge shotgun that he let me borrow on occasion. That allowed me to hunt in the nearby countryside for pheasants, quail, partridge, ducks, rabbits and squirrels. Can you imagine the protein addition to the previously mentioned cuisine? For even more protein, we frequently speared suckers, first cousins to carp, and other bottom feeders, in Bowman Creek. The exact venue was a spot Chuck had discovered, where that small body of water meandered past his grandmother's house. Suckers are bony fish with curved snouts. They have a slightly muddy taste but fit right in with the formerly popular saying that "beggars can't be choosers!".

You may wonder how it is that a six year old could be trusted with a shotgun. I readily confess that I don't recall the earliest date I went hunting, but it was more than likely not until I was nine or ten. There were no laws covering juvenile gunplay, at least none that I can remember. And this was a very small town. I don't think anyone had, or for that matter could even afford a hunting license. Harold Thompson, a local resident with absolutely no background in law enforcement was our village marshal. We were probably over-staffed with the one public safety official. I do not recall a single arrest. Harold might have made one or two, but you can be assured that they were not for hunting without a license!

A very clear recollection is that shotgun shells for a 410-gauge cost $1.00 for a box of twenty-five. My math-oriented mind quickly calculated that to be equivalent to four cents per shot. If you could grasp the idea of how paltry were my earnings at the time, you should have no problem in understanding how sure I was of probable success before I ever pulled the trigger. I have never been able to forget what grief it gave me to miss the intended target, and unfortunately that happened far too often.

If I got two rabbits on any given day one would be given to Chuck. He always returned this sort of favor, and I think I came out well ahead on this arrangement. There were two important reasons: Number one, he went hunting more often. And number two, he was a better shot!

CHAPTER 2
GRAVEYARD GOPHER HUNTING

Brooklyn Wisconsin, the village I lived in (population 406) became over-run with gophers for no apparent reason in 1934 when I was eight years old. The Village Council decided to pay five cents for each gopher that was eliminated, the proof of execution being a dismembered gopher leg. They had to have thought we were all idiots. Because we were not, we managed to collect twenty cents per gopher for quite some time. The politicians finally figured what was happening to cause the budget line item for gopher slaughter to be grossly underestimated. There was some talk among the town gossips that the Council might demand restitution for the scam, but cooler heads prevailed. It was decided that the rules would be changed to now require a right hind leg. Fortunately, the new measurement would not be applied retroactively.

The more enterprising among us briefly toyed with the idea that it might be somewhat difficult to distinguish a right hind leg from a left hind leg. But we finally settled on the theory that in due course such bold actions might well also be challenged, and that perhaps this time the restitution idea might be resurrected. And what the heck, Chuck and I were still able to make a quarter or fifty cents on a really good day, even living within the rules. After all, we were considered to be two of the most skilled gopher hunters in the entire town!

There were several methods available to the gopher hunters of the day. There was always a nearby water supply in the village cemetery, which was used to water the flowers on the graves. Since the local gopher population had elected to live amongst the tombstones in great number, the cemetery became one of our favorite venues for the hunt. Since water was readily available, drowning was the simplest and most economical approach. One would merely pour water in the hole until the gasping prey came floating out. Some hunters preferred a club as their weapon, while others preferred the BB gun approach; neither seems to require any further explanation.

A really fun technique was to obtain a long piece of strong cord and to put a noose around the hole. Then one needed to back off approximately ten feet and crouch. Next, whistling was required. A gopher possesses a vast amount of curiosity and will stick his head up from the hole in an attempt to determine the source of the whistling. Since I can't recall of ever hearing a gopher whistle, I am unable to explain the reason for this. It is but one of the many things Chuck taught me, and almost all of his pearls of wisdom produced excellent results.

It is necessary to be crouched low enough so that the prey cannot see you. Another short whistle causes the unwary rodent to rise a bit higher in a further attempt to observe the whistler. At precisely the right moment (a point of time which can only be determined from a great deal of practice) the hunter would yank on the cord. Voila! The cord tightened around the head, the body, or sometimes just one foot. But one thing was certain. The hunter was now five cents wealthier.

The leg was detached from the dead gopher by using a pocketknife, a tool possessed by every boy of that era. A pocketknife was essential for many things in addition to gopher hunting. Game had to be eviscerated and skinned, sticks required whittling, and mumblypeg was one of the favorite games for boys. Of course one needed to throw a knife at a tree trunk every now and then in order to demonstrate one's skill with the weapon. The severed gopher legs were put in a paper bag and stored in a cool place until the next City Council meeting, where the hunter presented them with understandable pride. Several mothers were upset at discovering a collection of gopher legs in their icebox. We did not have an icebox so I utilized a cool, dark corner of our cellar, which made Aunt Clara much happier than the afore-mentioned mothers. (Other than Mickey Mouse and perhaps Cinderella's coachmen, I don't think rodents have ever scored very well in women's evaluations.) Not in men's either if you really think about it.

By the way, cellars were cool because they were underground. If a cellar was located under the house, it might sometimes be called a basement. Some were totally concrete, while others had dirt floors. Still others were just excavations that had some sort of roof built over them. Since they were cool all year-round, they were used for food storage, especially home-canned fruits and vegetables, and fresh root vegetables like potatoes and carrots.

CHAPTER 3
FRUITS AND VEGETABLES

Rather early in life, probably by the age of eight or nine, I discovered that asparagus grew wild alongside country roads and at the sides of the railroad track that ran through our community. In the spring I watched for the new growth to appear. I then picked as much as could be found. On a good day, which one could define as a day that someone hadn't beaten me to it, it was quite easy to gather about four pounds. I gave roughly half of it to Aunt Clara to supplement our food supply. She boiled it in water to provide a fresh, nourishing and tasty treat. It gave me a great sense of pride to be able to make this contribution to our livelihood. As for the other two pounds, it was sold to a local grocery store. It was weighed on the store scale, and I was paid ten cents per pound. The more agile mind may have already calculated this day's "take" to be the equivalent of four gopher legs.

Large machines were not yet available to pick green string beans for the canneries, and every adult and child who wanted to be involved in this highly seasonal work was welcome. Many of my friends gave it a try but they all agreed with me that this "stoop labor" thing was not really for us.

One year, probably 1936 when I was ten, I decided that growing cucumbers for the pickle factory could be a good source of income. A lot of work went into this venture in the form of preparing the ground, planting, weeding, and especially the picking process. This was another example of labor requiring stooping. Nobody had warned me about how severely the factory personnel would perform the grading process. Perhaps I was a little bit paranoid, but it seemed that my harvest included a lot of inferior grade cucumbers. To make matters even worse, the price collapsed that season. The whole idea turned out to be a disaster for me. It probably would have been more productive if the time had been devoted to catching gophers.

One undertaking that turned out well was the picking of strawberries "on shares". Yes, it was more stoop labor and we didn't get paid in cash. However, when you picked two crates of berries, the grower kept the one that looked best to his practiced eye. The picker got to take the second crate home with him at no charge. We were able to eat a lot of fresh berries and the rest went into strawberry jam.

One sunny, spring day Chuck was at our house discussing his latest financial brainstorm. He happened to notice something growing wild in the unoccupied adjacent lot. "Hey look! That's horseradish", he exuberantly announced. Most of us would probably be surprised to hear that horseradish has been known for three thousand years. It has always been considered to have substantial medicinal qualities. Even today it is thought to be an effective diuretic, good for urinary tract infections, bronchitis, sinus congestion, ingrown toenails and coughs.

It is probably reasonable to assume that not very many people could recognize horseradish just after it peeked above the ground in the spring. And would any of us have a clue about that being the best time to harvest the tender roots? Chuck knew about all of this! I never thought to ask him why.

"Go get a shovel" Chuck ordered, as was his right as senior partner in all of our ventures. This "executive order" turned out to be the beginning of a potentially lucrative new business.

Under the very capable supervision of our leader, we dug up the roots and washed them, right after chopping off the green tops. Next, we removed the skins, paring them as you would a carrot or potato. The roots were then sliced into a workable size and run through a meat grinder to a fine texture. Some vinegar and a tiny bit of salt were added and this completed product was mixed thoroughly. The material was then spooned into used mayonnaise, pickle, and jam and jelly jars. These containers had been meticulously washed clean and dried. We went door to door selling our product. There were several sizes ranging from ten cents to a quarter. We made a fortune because our only expenses were the vinegar and salt, both of which were low cost items. And perhaps the greatest advantage came from not having to deal with the authorities at the Food and Drug Administration!

CHAPTER 4
THE FARM

Every year except one, between the ages of six and nineteen (1932-1945), it was my wonderful good fortune to live the entire summer on a small forty-acre farm. The farm was located one and one half miles northeast of Shell Lake, a city with a population of about one thousand. It was in northwestern Wisconsin, three hundred miles from Brooklyn and about half way between Eau Claire and Superior.

This fine opportunity was at the invitation of Margaret McNabb and her family. Margaret was a schoolteacher in Brooklyn for many years. She met my dad when I was five or six years old, and they became very close friends. She was my teacher in the fifth and sixth grades. Margaret was held in high esteem as a teacher, and thought to be quite strict. I agree on both counts! And, because of her relationship with my dad, she was extremely careful not to show me any special favor. The result was that I dearly loved her in the summer months, but not as much during the two winters when I was in her classes. At any rate, she loved me all year round and had a huge impact on my life. My appreciation is without bounds.

She was the second woman to give me an abundance of love, guidance and encouragement. Now, unlike my friends who had a living mother, I was blessed with two wonderful surrogates, who together very capably performed in that capacity. They both were, or had been schoolteachers. They certainly taught me a lot about life. It has probably already occurred to you that my summers "up north" gave my Aunt Clara a bit of a respite each year. I'm sure that she missed me a little, but for her it must have been a restful vacation.

Being involved with the McNabb family provided me with a third set of "grandparents". That may be slightly overstated because my two grandfathers had both died before I was born. So Charlie McNabb, Margaret's father became the first living "grandfather" I had known, and he was a wonderful source of joy and amusement for me.

For example, he could eat peas with a knife better than anyone else I ever knew. This involved the slight flattening of several peas at a time with a table knife and then balancing them precariously on the knife in order to transport them to one's mouth. It was nothing less than magic to watch, and was quite routinely performed by the elderly gentlemen of that era.

"Grandma", Maggie McNabb let me "help" her bake bread and taught me a lot of other fun things. One of them was separating cream from milk using a DeLaval cream separator. Another was making ice cream with an old-fashioned ice cream maker. I remember how difficult it was to turn the crank by the time the treat was almost finished, and what a delight it was to lick the dasher. Is it any wonder that I dearly loved both of my newly acquired "grandparents"?

In addition to the elder McNabbs and Margaret, the family also included another daughter, Janet, and four sons. The boys were named George,

Frank, Charles, Jr. (Max), and John. Frank and Max were married and lived nearby. George worked on the railroad and was frequently out of town during the week. John had a job in town and often came home late. It was because of this that I learned how to milk the cows by the time I was seven or eight years old. I was happy that they didn't have to pay someone else to do it. The "boys" would congregate on weekends to do the bulk of the farm work. "Grandpa" needed a cane the entire time I knew him. He was unable to provide much to the farming effort except good advice.

The first summer on the farm, at age six, one of my main chores was feeding the chickens. The second summer my responsibilities were expanded to include the gathering of eggs and the hauling of wood for the cook-stove. The wood was transported in a small wagon. Every summer, the list of my chores was expanded and the final two summers, 1944 and 1945 when I was 18 and 19, I ran the whole farm. That included plowing, planting, harvesting and everything else. At that time all of the McNabb brothers were either in the Armed Services or away at work.

The farm work included milking cows, slopping hogs, planting and cultivating corn, making hay, and you name it. And just imagine, there was not a tractor in sight. I believe I could still harness a horse if I had to, because I certainly had to harness old Bonnie and Dick a lot of times. But there was plenty of time for riding Bonnie, going fishing or swimming, hunting, or walking in the woods, or gathering blackberries, wild strawberries, blueberries, and gooseberries. Whatever the pleasures of a young man at that time, I was usually able to find the time for them in spite of working hard on the farm.

It's especially hard work to operate a one bottom walking plow behind a team of horses. I'd rather work with the riding equipment like the cultivator, the hay mower and the hay rake or the hay wagon. The horses didn't seem to have a preference unless it was the hay rake, which was the easiest for them to pull. I would say "gee" or "haw" to them, which in horse talk is "right" and "left". But more often than not they would ignore the verbal suggestions and I would have to resort to using the reins.

Tending to the garden was an important part of the farm work. Every year we plowed, disked, and harrowed about an acre of ground for the garden. First, the ground was prepared with a plow, drawn by a team of horses. The second operation entailed driving the horses as they pulled a piece of equipment with many parallel disks that pulverized the furrows of the plowed ground. That was what we called "disking". For "harrowing", the horses pulled a piece of equipment which had many spike-like projections that broke up the lumps and smoothed the garden surface.

The garden was then ready to be further smoothed with the use of a hand rake. Finally, it was staked and planted. We raised many different kinds of vegetables, the majority of which we canned in two-quart jars. These were stored down in the cellar. There were two large bins in the cellar. One was to store potatoes. The other was for carrots, which were put down in layers. Each layer was covered with a little bit of sand. The sand delayed spoilage throughout the entire winter.

By the end of the harvest, there were always acorn and hubbard squash and pumpkins hanging from the ceiling by a piece of binder twine tied to their stems. Hanging in the air kept them from spoiling for months. A very significant portion of the following winter's nourishment was preserved in that cellar.

The only fertilizer we ever used was aged manure from the animals.

And we never put chemicals on the land or the crops to kill insects or prevent diseases. I do have a vivid memory of picking off potato bugs by hand and dropping them into a can of kerosene. The products we produced on that farm would today be honestly labeled as organic, so I am happy to have been something of a "pioneer" in organic farming.

We mostly harvested hay to feed the cows, and corn to feed the chickens and pigs. Occasionally we would "take a flyer" on something like barley or rye. I don't recall that any of the flyers were especially successful and we would have probably been better off sticking to hay and corn.

To further support that theory, I must tell you of a venture in which I became involved. One day, George McNabb said to me "I was approached in town today, by a man proposing a joint venture having to do with squash. He wondered if we were interested. What do you think?" In retrospect I should have pleaded most anything to avoid the deal, but remember, I was an adventurous young man. "Yes, let's go for it" was my quick answer.

So the very next day I was visited by a crusty old gentleman from Shell Lake named George Bohn. Everyone in the area knew him and even I was aware that he had a reputation for lacking good judgment. But his proposition interested me and I honestly thought I might make a little money. Here was the deal: I was to plow, disk and harrow four acres of the McNabb farm. George Bohn would buy the squash seed and he and I would do the planting in accordance with his supervision.

I was also to do the cultivating. Perhaps a better word for cultivating is weeding. He and I were to harvest the crop and he was to market it. We would give the McNabb family a fair share for the use of the land, and then he and I planned to split the anticipated fat profits right down the middle. "What do you think?" he asked. "It sounds good to me" I replied.

Have you guessed yet? For all of that hard and time-consuming labor I received zilch. In fairness, I think that figure was equal to George McNabb's receipts. Oh, there were a lot of explanations offered. "It was such a bad market year. Our harvest was mostly sub-prime squash", etc. I'm not sure that any of the excuses were true. But in what is sometimes described as "the good old days", a kid didn't have much leverage in an argument with an adult.

The good news is that this experience was probably equivalent to one or two college courses in negotiating and dealing with others in matters of business!

The scariest farming task for me was cutting hay. I suppose it was the action of the sharp oscillating blades and the realization that if you were accidentally thrown in front of those blades, it would result in decapitation. Farming has always been a dangerous occupation and farm accidents are still frequent. Even without the powerful and unruly horses, bad things can happen. Every now and again I will read about a tractor overturning and crushing a farmer to death. Farmers with missing fingers or hands were a fairly common sight.

These days every dairy farmer has a milking machine. Back then, only our neighbor, Gene Banek, had one and the rest of us got milk from the cows the old-fashioned way. There were several summers when I milked from one to four cows twice a day, seven days a week. It was not all that difficult once you got the hang of it. One summer I worked for a month and a half helping a neighbor farmer. During that period, I milked eight cows twice a day.

Each time I milked the cows, the three or four farm cats would sit nearby watching me in eager anticipation. Sooner or later I would squirt milk in their direction. Only a small amount of milk actually hit their open mouths. Both the cats and I enjoyed the routine that followed, which consisted of the cats lapping all the rest of the milk from their fur.

Some farmers took all of their milk to the local creamery. We did that sometimes, but more often than not, because we could get more money for cream than milk, we separated at least a portion of the milk into cream and non-fat milk. The cream was sold to the creamery for the purpose of churning butter. We frequently set some aside for homemade ice cream. Turning the crank on the DeLaval cream separator to get it started was harder work than turning the crank on the ice cream maker to get it finished. So what happened to the non-fat milk? In those days, nobody ever considered drinking what was then known as "blue milk". It was fed to the calves and the hogs.

Membership in the 4H club between the ages of ten and sixteen was very important to me. Our club was called the Excella 4H Club and it is still in existence. The adult leader for many years was Janet McNabb. I entered a lot of things each year in the County Fair and earned a good bit of money from prize premiums. One year I entered the poultry-judging contest and won first place. One of the judges of that contest said to me: "Congratulations young man. You have earned a perfect score. That has never been accomplished by anyone before today." And the last time I checked, it still had never been done again.

At any rate, I won an all-expenses paid trip to the State Fair in Milwaukee to represent Washburn County. There I placed seventeenth out of seventy-one, which everyone thought was great. However, it was a great disappointment for me. I had memorized how to recognize every breed of chicken in the world. I was totally competent to pick the superior bird from a group, and could easily determine which hens were good egg layers and which were not. But they threw me a curve. I had no idea how to candle and grade eggs. It requires looking at an egg with a strong light behind it, weighing the egg, and assigning a grade based upon these observations, such as "Grade A Large". I'm convinced to this day that my lack of that knowledge cost me first place.

So how did I do financially with my farm work? The prize premiums at the fairs added up to a significant amount. My 4H projects also made a substantial amount of money for me in the market place. Notable among these were the poultry products. I sold a lot of eggs, but the "big money" was from the slaughtering, plucking, eviscerating and subsequent selling of the chickens. Raising cucumbers and squash were disasters in terms of labor, but only a small amount of money was lost, and that was for buying cucumber seed. The McNabb family provided my room and board and frequently shared the milk money with me. I always believed they treated me fairly and then some, and I will be forever grateful for their very significant contribution to my life.

I must relate a pig story before the farming chapter ends. One or two years after finishing my farming experience, I came home on leave from the war service. My dad said to me: "Follow me. I want to show you something." (He was taking care of the farm at that time.) He then ushered me to the pigpen, an area that always had in it a wooden trough for the feeding of slop. In case you are a city person, I hasten to explain that slop is a mixture of water (sometimes skim milk) and animal feed in the form of a mash. The latter is made from cereal grain that has been finely ground.

Pigs are impatient and voracious feeders and generally have at least two of their feet in the trough while the farmer is attempting to pour the slop. But I observed this scene in utter disbelief as my dad mixed and poured the slop with all four young pigs standing at rigid attention outside of the trough. At the end of our chat, my dad picked up a stick and faked hitting the side of the trough with it. The pigs flinched but quickly leaped back into formation. We talked a bit more, and at last he hit the side of the trough with the stick. At that moment the pigs leaped into action and started doing what pigs best like to do. They jumped into the trough and ate like pigs!

You may not be aware of the fact that pigs possess a lot of intelligence. But I never would have imagined that they could be trained to behave in this fashion. I often wondered if dad was a natural born animal trainer, or if he had taken massive amounts of time "tapping" the pigs with the stick to get their attention!

CHAPTER 5
A VENTURE INTO PUBLISHING

At about the age of ten, Betty Hansen, one of my classmates and I came up with the idea (this one wasn't Chuck's) that we could probably put out a weekly newspaper. Our town had a regular weekly newspaper named The Brooklyn Teller, and so to get some good input we went right to the source. Amazingly, the man responsible for the existing paper was not terrified by this great impending threat. On the contrary, he welcomed the competition and guided us through the entire process, explaining in detail what we needed. So classmates Bob Johnson and Harvey Smith joined with Betty and me, and the four of us wore many hats as we shared the responsibilities of publisher, editor, reporter, ad salesperson, subscription seller, and paper boy/girl.

This was an excellent source of knowledge about much of what goes on in the world of commerce. We learned the joy of coming across a news scoop, which we always happily shared with the existing newspaper. We learned the disappointment of being turned down for an ad or a subscription. We also had another lesson regarding hard work because this venture required a lot of it. Lastly, we learned a good deal about the payment of operating expenses, the collection of and accounting for ad revenues and subscriptions, and the sharing of the profits.

Our new paper was named The Weekly Reminder and true to its name came out once each week. It consisted of four pages approximately five inches wide and six inches high. It was always printed on colored paper, which was different than competing publications and made it easy to recognize. I guess the size also accomplished that! I recall that it sold for one or two cents per copy. Remember, this was in about 1936 when a dollar was a lot of money. As I recall, our production run was approximately fifty copies.

Our benefactor, wise in the ways of publishing, seemed to enjoy the publication of The Weekly Reminder every bit as much as we did. He was perhaps the most disappointed of all when our venture "folded" during the second year of its life. We had provided our reading public with nearly seventy interesting and provocative issues. The personnel who were there at the outset saw the project through and no additional people were hired. We all missed watching our mentor at work on the old linotype machine and I think he greatly missed the happy laughter of busy kids around the shop.

The only time I was ever unhappy with him was the day he asked me: "Have you ever seen Type Lice"? I replied: "No sir", so he said: "Let me show you one". He explained that: "You have to get very close to see them because they are so small". He had previously made a slight separation in the top of a row of lead slugs that had come from the linotype. Those slugs constituted a column-line of the newspaper. Into the gap he had poured a small amount of carbon tetrachloride, a liquid that feels very cold when it comes into contact with the skin. Since I could not yet see the Type Lice, I got my eye down to just above the gap. At the appropriate moment he rapidly closed the gap by pushing against the end of the row of slugs. The resulting cold splash into my face caused me to utter a loud profanity that absolutely delighted the experienced publisher. It took me a while to forgive him but eventually I did. Later in life I met a couple of Devil's Apprentices, the title given to the "gofer" in a print shop. They both confessed that they had been similarly introduced to Type Lice.

Harvey and I are the only members of this entrepreneurial group who are still alive. Due to his age, eighty-four compared with my eighty-three, his memory is understandably no better than mine but we agree that the newspaper business did all right for us.

CHAPTER 6
FISH BAIT AND PIGEONS

There was one idea I gave to Chuck. One spring, I noticed that there were a lot of frogs in a catch basin of the storm sewer. We fashioned a net from scrap wire, a long handle, and some gauze, all of which we found at the dump. After lifting the protective grate, not an easy task, we netted frogs and put them in a bucket. We had constructed a holding-pen out of scrap wood and chicken wire that we had also found in the dump.

Frogs make wonderful fish bait, especially for bass, and we had no trouble selling them to fishermen. My memory is fuzzy on the price, but I think we got twenty-five cents for a dozen frogs, and we had oodles of them.

There was a downside to this scheme. I had acquired from Aunt Clara a deadly fear of snakes, even harmless ones. Frogs are the favorite food of snakes. Ergo, there were always snakes hanging out near the pen. I had to exercise extreme caution at all times.

In the summertime, while living in Shell Lake, I put up a sign along the road that announced "Worms for Sale". I developed a great worm farm in the orchard, by keeping the ground moist and working used coffee grounds into the top inch or so of soil. The result was fat and happy worms and they made excellent bait.

The initial charge was twenty-five cents a dozen, and this price increased by degrees to fifty cents a dozen through the five or six years I worked at it. My very best customer was Bert Shipman, our local barber, who insisted on helping me dig, and therefore was in the best position to select the very fattest worms. It never did offend me, especially since he always overpaid.

There was an old abandoned icehouse about a block from our house in Brooklyn. Many pigeons had adopted it as their residence. Now it just might surprise you to learn that quite a few people were willing to pay ten or fifteen cents for a pigeon that had been killed, plucked and eviscerated. It didn't surprise Chuck!

At night, when they were roosting, he would climb up near the roof and wrap a leg around one of the rafters. From this precarious position, with the aid of a flashlight, he utilized a long wire with a crook fashioned at the end, to snag the roosting birds by the legs. He then wrung their necks and dropped them down to me. I started plucking and gutting the birds and Chuck joined me in that effort as soon as he had completed the hunt. We stored them in our cellars, and sold them door-to-door the next day. Some had been ordered in advance. We loved to have advance orders to fill.

Our harvest of the birds was timed to accommodate what is now known as "sustainability". The pigeons were given adequate time to do their thing in order to multiply. Because of our readings and observations of the ways practiced by the Native Americans, we never over-harvested our resources and accordingly, we never ran out of raw material for this venture.

Chapter 7
MY FRIEND THE DUMP

In the reading of this book you will occasionally see a reference to the "dump". This may not be a familiar term in your experience so I will attempt to clarify. You may know it as a disposal facility or a sanitary landfill. It now costs a small fortune to dump something and they are very fussy about what it is that you are dumping. Moreover, they may not even let you near the place, but insist you pay someone an arm and a leg to haul your stuff to the disposal location.

"In my day", as I like to refer to it while talking to my children, the dump was absolutely free. You could dump anything, including lead paint, used oil from your car, hydrochloric acid, old car batteries, and dead pets–absolutely everything! How's that for convenience? We were certainly oblivious to dangerous environmental issues that are so widely known about and discussed today. But by prowling through the refuse and gathering items to suit our needs, we were surely practicing recycling in our own personal way.

Even better, anyone who so desired could visit the dump at any time they wished, day or night, and carry off anything they wanted. It's possible that this arrangement was the source of the old adage that proclaims "one man's junk is another man's treasure". Through the years, the dump proved to be an absolute gold mine for Chuck and me.

I claimed ownership title to many treasures. However, one had to be very careful because the venue included a lot of broken, jagged glass and countless sharp metal edges. Mercurochrome was frequently needed for all sorts of cuts and scrapes. I don't think it was of much help to fight off infection, but it was the kids' overwhelming choice over tincture of iodine, which stung like crazy.

Copper-bottomed tanks were occasionally tossed, and it was a real coup if you found one before anyone else could zero in on it. The common usage for this item was the home laundry. Most of us did not have running water. We take it totally for granted in this day and age. But running water first became available to me when I arrived at college. Prior to that time, I was able to use the well at McNabb's farm. But in Brooklyn, we had to pump all of our water at our neighbor's well. This was then schlepped home and placed into the aforementioned copper-bottomed tank that had been put on top of the coal/wood-burning stove. When the water neared the boiling stage, it was scooped into the nearby wringer washer. I will assume that the reader may have seen such a device in a museum or perhaps at a county fair, so will not belabor you with a lengthy description of old-time wringer washers.

Back to the copper-bottomed tank, it was usually discarded because of a leak. Solder was of no use to repair them, because the heat from the stovetop melted the repair job. Sometimes, because copper is so malleable, you could get lucky with a hammer by beating the offending hole closed. At the very worst you could sell it to a junk collector. There were items gleaned from the dump that were far too numerous to mention here, but Chuck and I did very well in the scavenging business.

The dump was also a great place to hone your marksmanship skills by shooting rats. These varmints loved the place because there was plenty of garbage to eat, and lots of good places to hide. It also made a good place for the boys to have BB gun wars, because one could always find a good spot from which to shoot, like an old packing crate or a seat cushion from a car. Mothers, and in my case an aunt, were obviously completely unaware of these conflagrations. They would have had a hemorrhage. Can't any youngster just hear all the adults saying "you'll shoot your eye out, kid"?

CHAPTER 8
CARTING ASHES

Each winter the wood and coal-burning stoves and furnaces in use at the time, generated from two to eight bushel-baskets full of ashes and clinkers. The latter was the name for the unburned residue from coal. The residents would usually drop them in a pile in the back yard, most often in the area that was used for a summer vegetable garden. It was then necessary to remove them each spring, prior to the planting of the garden.

These annual accumulations looked like a real opportunity to Chuck. One day he found an abandoned cart at the dump and pulled it to his house for some much-needed repair. He explained the plan to me, and asked: "Can you come to my place and help me?" My reply, as usual, was: "When do we start?" The answer came as no surprise: "Now!"

The repaired cart would accommodate some twenty bushel-baskets, twelve of them in the bed of the cart, and four on each side attached with wire. All twenty were retrieved from the dump and were carefully repaired with parts cannibalized from other baskets found at the dump.

You may not be familiar with the bushel-basket, so I will attempt to describe it. It is roughly sixteen inches high, with about a fourteen-inch diameter on the bottom, tapering to about an eighteen inch-diameter on top. Its capacity, in keeping with its name, is a bushel. That is equivalent to four pecks or thirty-two quarts. It is constructed of thin slats of wood called "shuck", which is commonly used to make orange crates. And these were bound together with wire to form the basket shape. They were very common at one time, and were used to transport or store corn and other grains, freshly picked vegetables, feed for livestock, empty tin cans, old newspapers and many other things. "Why not ashes?" was Chuck's question.

We went door-to-door negotiating oral contracts to haul ashes to the dump, charging an average of ten cents per bushel-basketful. With a twenty-basket capacity, we could handle two large jobs or several small ones in a single trip. Fully loaded, the cart was difficult to manage for two young boys, one pulling and one pushing. Jobs in the southeast end of town were not bad because that's where the dump was located. So those trips were downhill or on the level. But jobs in the other three sectors presented a real challenge.

This turned out to be one of the most lucrative of Chuck's many schemes. Although highly seasonal in nature, it contributed a significant amount to our bank-savings-accounts, which were growing by leaps and bounds. On a good Saturday, we could handle four loads, which would generate seven or eight dollars. To show that this was a really good deal, let me present you with a basis for comparison. At that time an adult laborer could expect to be paid twenty-five cents an hour. That assumes he was fortunate enough to find a job.

For many years, Phillip "Scoop" Wackman was the bank President.

Although we were surely not his largest depositors, he always treated us as if we were. I think he was proud of us as young businessmen. The motto of the Brooklyn State Bank still rings in my ears: "A Good Bank in a Good Town". And it was!

Our savings accounts were increasing rapidly. The main reason was that our earnings greatly exceeded our basic needs. After all, a hamburger cost a nickel and a milk shake was a dime. And since Chuck and I were small for our ages, we could get into the two movie theaters in the neighboring town of Evansville for only a dime. That was true almost to the time of high school graduation. It was not until then that they started "carding" us.

I must digress for a moment, because the thought of a milk shake brings back a memory that my brother cherished. Observing it almost always caused him to laugh. Good old Mr. Dietz, the long-time proprietor of the drugstore in Brooklyn, was an old fashioned, slow moving man. The soda-fountain area of the drugstore was always very dimly lit. To make a milkshake, Mr. Dietz would first lift open the lid over the ice cream, and with his right hand, take the scoop from its container of rinse water. After that, he picked up a flashlight in his left hand. He then turned it on and pointed it down into the dark recess of the ice cream container. Next, he reached down deeply into the container and filled the scoop, lifted it from the depths, turned off the flashlight and laid it down. He then emptied the scoop into the tall, aluminum milk shake container. Following that, he rinsed the scoop until it was meticulously clean. He repeated the entire repertoire three or four times. If you had been able to witness this labor-intensive performance, I believe you would have been as amused as was my brother.

We continued the ashes and clinkers business for a number of years, until we both got part-time jobs. And at the end of it all, when I was about age 15, as you might have already guessed, we took the cart full of baskets, full of ashes and clinkers, to the dump and left it there, lock, stock and barrel!

CHAPTER 9
A LOVE AFFAIR WITH POULTRY

Even before I joined the Excella 4H Club at age 10, I was into chickens. Margaret encouraged me to get twenty-five one-day-old chicks at the beginning of each summer in Shell Lake. After I joined 4H, the number rose to one hundred.

The first few nights in a young chick's life are very important. It is essential that they be kept warm. In the typical barnyard environment, a mother hen performs that task. But these chicks came from the nursery, where they were the product of an industrial-strength incubator. It was therefore important that we replace the mother hen with heat from incandescent light bulbs.

It is also necessary to keep plenty of drinking water, and food in the form of grain mash available to your new "babies". Even then you could expect to lose one or two out of a batch of twenty-five. You just hoped that coccidiosis, a dreaded poultry disease, didn't make its appearance and wipe out your entire investment. A stricken chick was so pitiful to watch as it shriveled and died. Also, coccidiosis was extremely contagious. Recently I chatted with George Arscott, a fellow resident of our retirement community. He is a retired college professor, who taught courses in the management of poultry. He told me that this disease is now under control, and no longer the threat that it once was.

My specialty was Barred Plymouth Rock cockerels (future roosters). Now if you have seen one chick that is a day old, you have seen them all. The sexing process at that time was a carefully guarded secret that was known by very few. Most of us couldn't tell a boy chick from a girl chick. Even the experts missed once in a while. However, even when I was ordering a hundred at a time, the most pullets (future hens) that would appear in the course of time were one or two.

The chicks grew rapidly and each year for several years I asked the County Agricultural Agent to come out to the farm to caponize twenty-five of the birds. This required a slit under each wing and a snipping and removal of the testes. These birds then lost the aggressiveness that the normal rooster possesses. They matured to a weight of nine or ten pounds, while my average mature fertile bird weighed only five to seven pounds.

When the birds were ready for market, I would take orders from Donnelly's Grocery Store in Shell Lake. They generally ordered two or three birds a week. I would behead the bird, lower it into scalding hot water for a few seconds, and then remove it and shake it as dry as possible. Next, I would pick off the feathers, eviscerate it and deliver it to the store. I had other regular customers in addition to Donnellys. I don't recall the price I received, but the total proceeds exceeded the price paid for the chicks plus feed costs by quite a margin.

There were other benefits as well. I always seemed to win more than my fair share of cash premiums at the county fair. That was in recognition of my blue ribbon poultry. And in a previous chapter I told you about the free trip I won to the State Fair in Milwaukee. A lot of my neighbors patted me on the back for capturing seventeenth place out of seventy-two contestants. But I had gone there to win, and was more than a little upset that I had not. (Perhaps that is the sort of thinking that causes my wife Grace to tell me I'm kind of competitive!)

The poultry business has really changed through the years. The competition in the industry has maintained both eggs and chickens as good bargains in our shopping for protein. The size of the individual operation today is principally responsible for this. The appropriate term to explain this is "the economy of scale".

Several years ago I attended a high school reunion in Brooklyn. Waldo (Duke) Disch, one of my old classmates, approached me and asked: "Would you be interested in buying my poultry business?" I replied: "How many birds do you have?" He responded: "I have ninety-three thousand leghorn hens". My answer to him was: "I wouldn't touch an operation with less than a half million birds". He smiled and said to me: "You really know something about this business, don't you"! I have never lost my fondness for chickens, and just last year located and purchased four chicks for my grandson, Connor. The acquisition comprised two Buff Orpingtons and two Silver-Laced Wyandottes.

The afore-mentioned George Arscott has updated me on a great deal of poultry knowledge. I had recently commented to someone that I resented eggshells being so thin, because of sanding the shells to clean them. He overheard the comment, and told me: "There is now an alternative approach. The shells may be cleaned through a washing process." I then asked him: "Are ground oyster shells still fed to laying hens in order to provide calcium?" He responded: "It is an element that is necessary for the development of the shell. It is still being done, especially for birds kept outside of cages."

To conclude this chapter, I want to let you know that my poultry was all "free-range". This was not due to any "political correctness" on my part. Rather, it was because the technique of raising birds in cages was not yet developed. As a result, I was not able to charge a higher price, as is now the case. In spite of that, I'm glad I raised my chicks where they had the freedom to run in the yard.

CHAPTER 10
AN ADVENTURE WITH PORK PRODUCTION

The local stockyard was quite close to our home in Brooklyn. It was a most interesting place and as a seven or eight-year-old boy I used to hang around there a lot. Farmers would bring their cows, calves, sheep and pigs to the stockyard in trucks, and unload them into designated pens, after first herding them over the scale for weighing purposes.

Jake Frei, the operator of the place took a liking to me. One day, when a farmer unloaded a sow with her litter, he grabbed the runt pig, handed it to me and said: "What about taking this little guy and fattening him up for me"? I quickly replied "Sure", with nary a thought about the consequences. Even though the runt pig weighed only ten pounds or so, Aunt Clara was not a happy camper when I arrived home with it.

It was not easy to convince her that this was a good thing, but somehow I did. The little guy was tethered to a tree trunk while I hammered together a proper sty out of some old boards I had found at the dump.

The next few weeks I cared for my charge as you would care for a newborn child. I fed it whatever scraps Aunt Clara could provide.

Potato peelings were the biggie. I was like a young Sherlock Holmes in finding cobs of corn that had spilled from farmers' wagons on the way to the feed mill.

This routine continued for two or three months. The end came the day Aunt Clara advised me that the squealing, and the newly discovered strange odor in the neighborhood were no longer welcome. The ultimatum was clear to me. The very next day I advised Jake: "We have a problem. My aunt says I have to get rid of the pig". His response reflected a deep understanding. "That's not really much of a problem. Just bring the pig back at your earliest opportunity."

In the life of an eight-year-old boy, it presented a perfect solution to the problem. However, I must confess a certain close relationship had already developed between boy and swine. One would think that in these circumstances I would have given my little friend a name. For the life of me, I am unable to recall whether I did or not. But I'm pretty sure that had I been able to ask Walt Disney for advice, he would probably have recommended "Porky"!

The next morning I returned the pig, and after running it across the scale Jake paid me the going rate, which amounted to sixty-five cents. That was pure profit since my total investment had been zero. Even so, except for that which might be required at the McNabb farm, it was to be the last time I would venture into the glamorous world of pork production!

Chapter 11
MURDERING FLIES FOR FUN AND PROFIT

Throughout my childhood, I did a lot of what was referred to as "errands" and "odd-jobs". An example of the former would be an elderly lady asking me to go to the grocery store for her. Examples of the latter classification would include such tasks as raking leaves, mowing lawns, and clearing the snow from sidewalks.

Perhaps the very oddest of odd jobs came from my Aunt Emily, Frank McNabb's wife. During two summers in Shell Lake, she hired me to swat flies. Her house was beleaguered with the pests. Perhaps it was the result of tomatoes rotting in the garden, which was right next to the house. Or maybe the house had been built a little too close to the barn. It may have been partially due to the fact that the house seemed always to be full of clutter.

Whatever the reason, I have never seen so many flies in one house in my entire life. So on several occasions, over the course of the two summers, I was engaged to swat flies. The employer provided the only essential tool, a fly swatter.

Compensation was to be in the amount of one penny for each fifteen flies that were dispatched. Aunt Emily said to me: "I think the amount is fair. What do you think?" I answered: "I think it is more than fair for doing something that is fun!" "You will also have the task of keeping track of the count", she added. Since the deal was going to be based on what we all know as "the honor-system", it was very important to me that the count be accurate.

To aid me with that assignment, I used paper and pencil to produce a small vertical mark for each of the first four flies in a batch. The fifth dead fly would be represented with a slanted line, drawn across the vertical marks. When a grouping of three of these formations had been registered, the resulting graphic presentation reflected, as Benjamin Franklin would have stated it, "a penny earned".

You can't get rich from a deal like this, but a young boy of eight or nine could do pretty well for himself, assuming he was in the right environment. From the perspective of an entrepreneur, there is an inherent pleasure in doing this kind of work. The risk of injury is minimal, and in an hour or so of swatting, it was possible to clear a nickel of pure profit. The only down side came from having to sweep the floor in order to dispose of the *corpora delicti*! This source of funds was to come to an abrupt end, when Uncle Frank and Aunt Emily moved away.

CHAPTER 12
THE PAPER ROUTE

Much of my income was produced by work that was highly seasonal in nature. Snow shoveling in the winter, spading gardens and ash hauling in the spring, mowing lawns in the summer and raking leaves in the fall are good examples of this. I longed for something "steady" so as to have some income that I could rely on all year long. My needs for things like hamburgers, movies and bowling were not seasonal in nature. Hence, there was a clear need for a year around source of "ready cash".

You can imagine my joy in discovering, at about the age of ten, that a paper route was available. After an exhausting interview, the man from the Capitol Times in Madison selected me for the job. My clientele at the start totaled sixteen subscribers but I soon built the number to twenty or more. I was to receive two cents for delivering each daily paper and five cents for each Sunday paper. Those rates were to increase dramatically over the next seven years that I held the job. The depression ended during that period of time and a degree of inflation occurred. My clientele averaged about twenty subscribers.

It was understandably necessary for me to arrange for a substitute carrier for every day during the summer, because I was in Shell Lake. A substitute was also needed at other times, when I was ill or otherwise indisposed. I was very successful in accomplishing this, except for one memorable occasion.

My high school baseball team, for which I was the second baseman, had gone on a school bus from Brooklyn to the near-by village of Juda for a game. Their field was in a pasture, so "sliding into third" was sometimes an entirely accurate description of the situation.

At approximately four p.m. that day, we were in the third inning of the game, locked in a close battle. My mind was cluttered with the requirements of my stellar play. Further, there is a great deal of excitement involved in a hotly contested game. In spite of it all, I was suddenly struck by an awful realization. My precious paper route was in rather immediate need of delivery. Somehow, I had not remembered to make the appropriate arrangements.

An understanding coach put me in touch with the Principal of Juda High School. "Follow me to my office" he said. After a short walk, we arrived at his office. He handed me his personal phone and I immediately called Aunt Clara. She promised to solve the problem, but only after giving me some well deserved criticism. If this incident were to occur in this modern time, I would simply grab my cell phone and by-pass the "middlemen" and the attendant criticism. But that was obviously not possible during the "days of yore", as my children like to refer to it.

However, that experience was to give me a moment of great joy many years later. While chatting one day with Roger Thompson, a good friend whom I had known for several years, we made a delightful discovery. He is the son of the school Principal who had come to my rescue in Juda so many years ago!

A paper route provided some really valuable experience for a young person. It required a good sense of responsibility. The job offered one an education in the collecting, accounting for, and remitting of money. Perhaps the most important experience came from the necessity of close dealings with people. Most of my customers accepted the fact that nobody is perfect, and that once in a while a boy's toss from a speeding bicycle might miss the porch and land in the bushes.

Mr. Wilson, however, was unforgiving. In order to satisfy him, I had to stop, put my bike on the kickstand, and climb the steps to the Wilson's front porch. Following that, I was required to carefully insert the paper in a holder on the wall. He seemed to take great pride in the fact that he had designed and built the holder. I suppose that his insistence for special consideration was not entirely unreasonable in the circumstances. None-the-less, it cost me about a minute of my time every day. That minute was vitally important in the life of a young boy, as it might better have been spent playing ball, shooting marbles or even daydreaming.

A paperboy also had to deal with the "slow-pay" problem. This was more likely to occur during that period of financial difficulty. We had to remit on a timely basis, even though the customer did not pay. One customer "stiffed" me, and his three months in arrears had to be paid out of my earnings. I learned a lot from that experience.

CHAPTER 13
THE BIG SNOW

While I was attending Brooklyn High School, perhaps during my sophomore year, we experienced a huge snowstorm. To make matters even worse, it arrived on the heels of what had already been an extraordinarily snowy winter season. So now there were almost two feet of fresh snow, on top of an already existing snow-pack of nearly four feet in unplowed areas.

The village put out a call for any able bodied person, who was willing to assist in snow removal. I immediately provided them with my name, and they assigned my good friend Bryant Wackman and me, to assist a man in loading snow onto a pickup truck. We shoveled snow for several days, and moved many truckloads of the white stuff from downtown, to a disposal area outside of town.

"Minimum Wage" was not a familiar term in those days. It is my recollection that what we were paid was pretty minimal. Whoever said "hard work never hurt anyone" must not have shoveled much snow! The resulting aches are indeed painful.

This same much-cursed snow, on the contrary, provided a lot of joy for a child. Throwing snowballs, making snowmen, building forts of snow, and playing the game of Fox and Goose were all loads of fun. The latter could best be described as "confined tag". Before play could begin, the players trampled a giant circle in the snow. The circle had a circumference of perhaps one hundred feet. The trampled area had a width of about one foot. Next, the circle was divided into two equal halves by further trampling of the snow. One of the players was then designated as being "it". He or she would attempt to tag another player. That accomplishment made the tagged player the new "it". All players were required to stay within the trampled boundaries. Breaching this regulation resulted in the offending participant immediately becoming "it".

Perhaps even better than the aforementioned pursuits, were cross-country skiing, sledding and tobogganing. However, there was one activity I enjoyed much more than any of those. In that era, following heavy snows, most farmers drove sleds. The sled had wooden runners and was drawn by a team of horses. The farmers used these vehicles to bring the milk to town, and to carry groceries and cattle feed back to the farm. We requested permission from a farmer to ride home with him. We then hitchhiked back to town on another sled. The process might even be repeated with other farmers if time allowed.

There was one danger to be avoided at all costs. Woe to the young boy or girl who was faced with the miscalculation of having ridden too long of a distance out of town, late in the day. Sometimes, we were unable to find another farmer heading into town, in order to hitch a ride back. There is nothing quite like a long walk on a cold winter day, to help you hone your ability to estimate time and distance!

Chapter 14

HIRED HAND

During the summer of the year I turned fifteen, a neighbor who farmed nearby approached me. He asked: "Would you be able to help me for one month? It is the height of the haying season and I really do need some assistance". I answered: "Yes, I can do that, but first I will have to get permission from the McNabbs." He readily understood, and said: "I'll keep my fingers crossed", a further indication of how desperate he was for some help. The McNabbs were quick to bless the arrangement, making both Mr. Davies and me happy. I could now make some extra money, while working for a person I really liked.

Will Davies was of Welsh stock, a God fearing man in his fifties. His greatest virtues were his kindness and his love of hard work. The workdays of that memorable month were to be long and demanding. I arose at five-thirty and did my morning chores at the McNabb farm. At that time, those could be done in an hour or an hour and a half at the most.

The distance between the two farms was about a mile. Although I had a bicycle at my Brooklyn home, a hand-me-down from my brother, I never had one at Shell Lake. So it was necessary to walk to the new job. Upon arrival, I helped Mr. Davies finish his chores. This most often meant that I would milk four more cows. This was accomplished by hand, of course. As I previously noted, only one farmer in the vicinity owned one of those new-fangled milking machines!

We then went to the house to partake of a "second breakfast". It was customary to have had some cereal, a cup of coffee and perhaps a piece of toast shortly after getting out of bed. The purpose of that was to bolster you for morning chores. Second breakfast generally included eggs, meat, fried potatoes, toast, a lot of coffee and perhaps a piece of cake or pie. It was not at all unusual to substitute (or add) pancakes once or twice a week.

Then, without further ceremony, it was off to the hay fields. Haying in those days consisted of mowing, drying, raking, shocking, and loading the hay onto a wagon. The hay was then placed in an outdoor stack or put in the barn. Mowing was done with a mowing machine pulled by a team of horses. The first day of this new employment found me helping to harness the team, and then doing some job like repairing fences or chopping down Canadian Thistles, the bane of the farmers in that area.

Meanwhile, Mr. Davies was out mowing hay. It then had to dry for a day or two. During that period, we worked together on other farm projects or he mowed hay in another field. He never allowed me to operate the mower, although I was already something of a veteran at the task. But my experience had all been acquired with a different team of horses. Every team has its own personality, and at times can be quite obstinate. At other times, one or both of the horses can be downright ornery. At any rate, extreme caution must be exercised. If a person were to fall into the path of the rapidly oscillating sickle blades, they could easily be killed.

The hay was then left to dry for a day or two. The next task was to rake the hay with a dump rake. This was a horse-drawn machine with about a dozen large, curved steel forks that were parallel. When the forks had scraped an ample amount of hay from the ground, you kicked on a pedal. That would "dump" the hay back onto the ground. We did our best to place the dumped batches end-to-end, thereby creating a windrow, which was the name given to a relatively straight line of material. Mr. Davies and I alternated with that task. Upon the completion of a windrow, one would use the dump rake to make individual piles (shocks), hence the name "shocking". It was then time for one man to "pitch" the shocks up onto the hay wagon, and for the other man to distribute it evenly on the wagon. Both of these tasks required the use of a pitchfork.

The final step in haying was to store it until it was to be used. If this was done in an outdoor stack, one man pitched the hay from the wagon and the other man distributed it evenly in building the stack. If the hay was to be stored in the barn, there were several methods available at the time. The simplest, but most physically demanding, was to pitch it from the wagon through the upper barn door, with the use of a pitchfork

The other two methods at the time were known as "slings" and "fork". In the former instance, one had to put a sling made of rope on the hay wagon, under the hay. The sling was then hoisted into the hayloft with ropes pulled by a team of horses, and utilizing a system of rails and pulleys that were located in the hayloft.

With the use of the other method, you pointed the sharp tines of a large steel fork down into the load of hay and then jumped on it with all your weight. It literally grabbed a large amount of hay, which was then hoisted in the same manner as with the sling.

That may be more than you ever wanted to know about olden methods of "making hay". They are all now archaic and have been replaced by either baling or simply chopping the hay. In the former, a tractor pulls a machine that cuts the hay and presses it into a bale or a roll. When using the other method, a tractor pulls a machine that cuts and pulverizes the hay, and then blows it into a covered wagon that is pulled behind.

I will conclude my treatise on haying with a final comment. No matter which of the three ancient methods was used, it was necessary for someone to go up into the hayloft, and mow (rhymes with cow) it away. That was the term for strewing it around, in order to achieve maximum storage volume. And the hay had better be very dry, because the spontaneous combustion resulting from moist hay was responsible for the burning down of many barns.

This chapter comes to an end with another anecdote. As previously mentioned, Mr. Davies was a God fearing man. I never heard him utter a single swear word. One day he and I were repairing the water tank from which the livestock drank. Suddenly, he accidentally hit his thumb a mighty blow with a hammer. Now, I thought, at long last I will hear a cuss word or two, which have been stored up for years. Here in print is the sum total of what gushed forth from his lips: "OUCH, GOLLY OUCH"!

After that long month of hard work, payday finally arrived. Remember that after each day in the fields and after helping Mr. Davies with his evening chores, I still had to walk home and do my own evening chores. So I was hoping that he would be generous. We frequently worked in the field until nearly sunset, which was around 9:30 at that time of the year. I must say I was more than a little unhappy when he said he was giving me sixty-five cents a day. That was, of course, in addition to all I cared to eat at second breakfast and at the big noon meal. I had really hoped for seventy-five cents a day. I must admit that I was bitterly disappointed! As a lesson, however, it was a good one. NEVER agree to do a job without first establishing what you will be paid.

CHAPTER 15
PRE AUTOMATION BOWLING PIN SETTER

At about age ten, I became aware of summer bowling leagues in Shell Lake. It looked like a good possibility to make some money. That was well before the introduction of automatic pin setting machines. In those days, if you didn't like the pin alignment, there was no reset button to push. It was, however, necessary to shout the word "reset". That usually did the trick.

I say usually, because the work was then done manually and there were times when the human being who was doing the job might be lollygagging. If a second shout failed to get results, the bowling alley proprietor would personally walk to the end of the alley to issue a sound tongue-lashing. "How would you like to get fired"? This utterance in a loud and angry voice seemed to always solve the problem.

The proprietor of the bowling establishment in Shell Lake was Peter Mahringer. He had been born in Germany and had a reputation for running a smooth operation. So the last thing in the world a kid ever wanted was to be the cause of Mr. Mahringer having to walk the length of the alley. His bad mood on such an occasion was legendary.

In spite of these infrequent occurrences, the job was popular because it paid relatively well. The pinsetters would almost always choose to set "double". This is somewhat the equivalent of a golf caddy who carries "double" by lugging the clubs of two golfers at the same time. In bowling, it meant that the setter of the pins handled two alleys at a time.

The compensation of a human pinsetter was a nickel a line. A line is defined as a game. A game is ten frames for one person. A frame is the rolling of two balls, one at a time. If you knock down all of the pins with the first ball, it is called a "strike", and you don't get a second ball. In league bowling, there were five bowlers on a team and they bowled three lines during a typical competition. Therefore, five bowlers times three lines is fifteen, times two teams equals a total of thirty lines. At a nickel a line, one could make a dollar and a half in two or three hours in an afternoon or evening. That was excellent income back then, so I set pins whenever I could.

The business end of a bowling lane is called a pit. The job required you to jump back and forth between the two pits. The trick was to be working in the pit where a bowling ball wasn't heading your way at the moment. It didn't take a lot of experience to get the hang of this. To be most effective, you had to jump down into the pit right after a ball arrived. You would then pick up the ball and place it in the ball return rack. Next, you would pick up the downed pins and put them in the pin rack. When all ten were in the rack, or it was the bowler's second ball in that frame, it was time to push down on the handle and the pins were reset. At that time, depending on the circumstances, you either jumped into the other pit to work or jumped up to sit on the shelf in the back of the pit in order to grab a moment of rest.

Very early in a pinsetter's career, he learned to pick up five pins at a time, two in each hand and one squeezed in between. It was hard on the knuckles and dropping a pin on one's foot can be more than a little bit uncomfortable. A pin is made of hard rock maple wood, which is then covered with plastic, paint and a hard glossy finish. It is 15 inches high, 4 3/4 inches wide at the widest point and weighs 3 pounds, 6 ounces. Both alertness and caution were required in dealing with these wooden missiles.

It isn't rocket science to recognize the result of a strike or a spare. But you needed to keep track of whether it was the bowler's first or second ball. This was usually pretty obvious, because if there were already some pins in the rack you could assume that it was the bowler's second ball that was coming down the alley. But what if the first ball had been a gutterball? And setting double increased the degree of difficulty in keeping track of the proceedings. Once in a while you realized you had erred, when you heard the loud voice of an irate bowler yelling: "Hey, wake up down there!"

We all hated to see the arrival of a macho young male bowler, who always threw the ball as hard and as fast as he could. This resulted in pins flying all over the pit. A flying pin hitting any part of the body produces pain. We had to be especially careful to avoid that. Even in normal circumstances, if you were sitting and resting in the back of the pit where the ball was arriving, it was necessary to raise your legs high up into the air.

If I were ever asked to design a fitness program, I would surely base it on the motions made by a person who had been a pinsetter. It was equivalent to bending over and touching your toes about a thousand times within a two to three hour period. To that one may add a total estimated weight lifted of about four tons of ball weight and over a ton of pin weight. Pushing down on the handle of the machine three hundred times is also good exercise. Add to that, the jumping back and forth between pits and jumping up onto the back shelf for some rest. Finally, quite a lot of hand/eye coordination was required to get it right every time.

The automatic pin setting machines in use today are expensive. However, over their lifetime of use, they undoubtedly cost less than human pinsetters. It is now possible for the proprietor to avoid payroll taxes, insurance costs, workers' comp, and probably an occasional lawsuit. I agree that progress is generally a good thing, but once more it has resulted in the demise of some pretty good jobs.

Chapter 16
THE FEED MILL

In 1941, at age fifteen, I applied for a part-time job at the local feed mill in Brooklyn. The Borst family owned the business. They had occasionally hired me as a baby sitter. The pay rate was twenty-five cents an hour, to baby-sit Roger (Buzz) Borst, who was four or five years younger than I. Perhaps that is why they hired me at the mill, as they knew me to be dependable.

I was paid in cash once a week. The pay envelope showed the deductions from gross earnings, such as unemployment tax and social security. One payday we were all shocked to see a new deduction. It was called the Victory Tax. This was soon after our entry into World War II. The people were assured by the federal government that it was to be strictly temporary and would be discontinued at the end of the war.

Surprise, surprise! At the end of the war it was not discontinued. But the name was changed. You know it today as the Withholding Tax! So there in a nutshell is the reason that at a fairly early age, I began to develop a healthy skepticism relating to the promises of government.

The work at the mill was hard. It consisted mainly of two tasks. The first was the manual unloading of railroad cars, which were full of sacks of corn, oats, or prepared cattle feed. The sacks weighed between eighty and one hundred pounds. You had to lift each one and stack them five high on a small pushcart. You then wheeled the cart to the appropriate place inside the mill and stacked the bags five high.

The second major task was to unload railroad cars full of coal. This was accomplished with a scoop shovel. The coal was shoveled onto a chute that terminated in a warehouse coal-bin. This was not only hard work, but it was dirty work, especially when bituminous, so-called "soft coal" was involved. "Hard coal", anthracite was much more expensive but was substantially cleaner burning. The use of it left much less residue and produced less smoke. One did not get as dirty handling the latter. But the added expense to customers was rather prohibitive and therefore reflected far fewer sales.

We were frequently the recipients of a visit from Bill Borst, Sr. He was Buzz's grandfather and one of the owners of the mill. He would join us at the work scene and lift or shovel rapidly. Since he was much older than the rest of us, we would speed up the work in order to keep pace with the "old man", the name by which we referred to him in privacy. But he always disappeared after a very short time. His goal, of course, was to get us to speed up the work. But we soon caught on and the work resumed its normal pace immediately after Bill Sr. was out of sight.

I really enjoyed this job and made good money. The hours were after school (and the paper route) and all day Saturday. I learned how to operate the grinding machinery, sack animal feeds, and how to quickly tie the top of a sack with a binder twine knot (clove hitch). I also enjoyed loading a ton of coal on a truck to deliver to customers. We would first open a basement window in the home. A chute was then placed between the truck and the open window. The coal was shoveled onto the chute and it slid down into the coal bin.

The feed mill job continued until graduation from high school and I will be forever grateful to the Borst family for the opportunity.

"Little Buzz" passed away shortly after his retirement, just a few years ago. I was fortunate enough to have had a nice visit with him in Bend, Oregon when I was traveling around the country in a motor home. That little squirt of a kid had earned a doctorate in geology and had enjoyed a successful career with Phillips Petroleum at their headquarters in Bartlesville, Oklahoma. His sister, Roma, studied Spanish at the University of Wisconsin and became widely known and greatly respected in academia as an outstanding teacher of the Spanish language.

CHAPTER 17

THE CREAMERY

Shell Lake had a creamery to which the local farmers sent the milk produced by their dairy cattle. Some of them had already run some of it through a cream separator. The creamery churned the cream into butter and dehydrated the milk.

During the two summers following my final two years in high school, I worked forty hours a week at the creamery. The major part of my job was operating the milk-dehydrating machine. This job made me a pretty busy person, because by then I was also fully in charge of running the McNabb farm.

The milk-dehydrator was an interesting machine. The milk was piped into the space between two hot rollers, revolving counter-clockwise to each other. This resulted in a thin layer of solid, dried milk accumulating on each roller. As these rollers came around to the outside position, a knife the length of the roller on each side skinned the thin layer of milk from the roller. That caused sheets of dried milk to billow from the machine. The product went down into a metal trough on both sides of the machine. It was pushed to the front of the machine by means of large, screw-like attachments. There it was reduced to powder by the blades of a hidden hammer mill. Finally, the powdered milk would drop into a wooden barrel that contained a large, waxed paper bag liner.

The old timer who taught me the rudiments of the job always had a cigar between his lips, no matter what he was doing. This disgusting prop might be lit or unlit at any given moment, but the other end was always soggy with saliva. While demonstrating the use of a pocketknife between the roller and the blade, which was needed in order to maintain the billowing effect, the soggy butt dropped into the trough containing the dehydrated milk.

My instinct was to try to grab it, but that might well have cost me the loss of my hand in the machinery. The old codger raced to the barrel and was able to retrieve a small amount of dark material, but the bulk of it was destined to remain in the barrel. Someone once told me that if you ever watched food being processed, you would probably never want to eat again. That sounds way too drastic, but as a minimum, we should all be wary of drinking a glass of dried milk with a hint of tobacco flavor!

Getting back to the process, you will remember that the milk powder was being collected in lined wooden barrels. Each filled barrel had a gross weight of nearly two hundred and twenty-five pounds. One of the requirements of the job was to put the heavy, paper liner in the barrel, and then weigh the barrel, including the wood top and the steel top ring. This information was then stenciled on the barrel top, using a marker pen. Later, when the gross weight was determined, that weight would also be recorded. The tare weight, determined by deducting the first weight from the second, was then entered on the barrel top.

An ongoing task was to ensure that the billowing effect of the milk coming off the machine rollers was constantly maintained. As previously mentioned, this was best accomplished by running a pocketknife along the area where the blade met the roller. Under normal circumstances, this had to be done every few minutes.

When the barrel was almost full to the top, you had to quickly roll that barrel out of the way, and replace it with another one that had been lined and weighed. The full barrel was then tilted a bit and rolled the rest of the way to the scale.

The liner top was twisted and tied with twine. Then the top was put on and the ring was put in place. A few small nails were driven through the ring, through the barrel stave and into the edge of the top. The gross weight was determined and the appropriate information entered on the top. Then came the hard part of the job. The barrels were stacked to a level of two barrels in height. Wrestling the heavy barrels to the second level required a gargantuan effort. Fortunately, farm work makes a person strong.

The best benefit on this job was the opportunity to go to the area where refrigerated milk was nearing the machine. There you were able to catch a cool, cool cupful. What a wonderful treat that was, especially on a hot summer day.

Our supervisor was a fun guy named Gilbert Linton. "Gib", as he was known, was a joy to work for but was somewhat indelicate in language and manner. I will refrain from freaking you out by relating any of his stomach-churning antics, but you may gather a feeling for the man from one of his favorite phrases. No matter how delicate a repair job we were engaged in, he would always yell out in a voice you could hear a mile away: "Hey, someone bring me a pipe wrench and a maul." These tools would be giant overkill for whatever task we were doing, but it was a pretty good indication of his personality. Old John Barleycorn, our pet phrase for whiskey, apparently got to Gib and he left us years ago. I shall always remember him with great fondness.

Every day at the end of the shift, it was customary to stop at a tavern for some refreshment. Walt Ek, the owner of the establishment, would sell all of us a beer or cocktail. That was true even though Herbie Swanson and I were well under the legal age, which was twenty-one at the time. But he drew the line at the second round. The two of us were always denied a second drink. However, we still got a kick out of yelling to the bartender and making a circular motion with the index finger extended and pointed down, the universal sign for ordering another drink for "all hands".

My friend Herbie was one of those unfortunates we used to label as "accident-prone". It was seldom that he was able to finish a shift without the need for at least one or two bandages. An incident occurs to me that may help you better understand his condition.

Near the end of each summer, it was customary for the management to take the crew to Ted Haag's Sarona House for a magnificent steak dinner. On one such occasion, shortly after we had entered our orders, Herbie excused himself and departed for the restroom. By the time he returned, we had already been served. As he approached the table, instead of returning to his seat in the normal manner, he swung one leg up over the top of his chair with a great flourish, and dropped into the chair with a mighty thud. He then picked up his knife and fork to attack his steak and accidentally drew the serrated knife across the back of his other hand that was holding the fork. The resulting bloody gash required a great deal of first aid and drew a lot of attention from the other diners.

Alas, the creamery was torn down years ago and is now a parking lot across from the hospital and behind the county buildings. But the experience of working there provided me with some precious memories, and a newly acquired expertise that prepared me for another job that I was to have in the near future. It also paid me the handsome sum of thirty-five cents an hour, which at that time could purchase quite a lot. A bag of popcorn at the Thursday night free movie in the park cost only a dime, and gasoline was a mere twenty cents a gallon. That was in 1942 and 1943, with WW2 gaining momentum in Europe.

CHAPTER 18
DELIVERING ICE

Although my involvement in the ice business only lasted two weeks, it is included here in the hopes that it may be of interest to you, and if you are older, it will probably bring back some memories.

I believe I was thirteen years old at the time and was spending another summer at the McNabb farm in Shell Lake. The man who delivered ice door to door wanted to go on a trip, so his assistant was to take over for that period. He needed a helper and I was approached as a likely prospect. Margaret was apprehensive, because the man I would be helping was Dode Bergen, the town drunk. Dode would be doing most of the driving. For reasons that were never quite clear to me, but perhaps because of my pleadings and assurances that I would be very alert to possible dangers, she finally gave her permission.

The Jacobs family had established the business many years earlier and now Charley Jacobs ran the show. The facility was housed in a large barn-like structure close to the lake. People could instantly recognize it as an icehouse, as there were always prodigious piles of sawdust near the building. Inside the icehouse, each piece of ice was well insulated because it was completely surrounded by sawdust.

In the winter, after the lake had frozen to a depth of several feet, massive chunks of ice were removed from the lake with the use of ice-saws and tongs. Although the process lacked preciseness, an effort was made to have each of the chunks weigh approximately four hundred pounds.

The chunks were pulled up to the edge of the icehouse using huge tongs and a team of horses. They were then pulled inside with tongs and a rope running through a series of pulleys. After they were placed in an appropriate location, they were surrounded on all four sides with sawdust. Melting was not a problem during the winter, but on a hot summer day the insulation was an important and necessary feature of the operation.

Refrigerated railroad cars were loaded out of the icehouse and ice was delivered to Chicago, Milwaukee, Madison and Minneapolis-St. Paul. The business flourished right up until the time of commercial refrigeration and ice-making machines. The earliest American refrigerator I can recall seeing was manufactured in 1929. But in rural Wisconsin, it was not until the 1950's that the majority of residents were able to own one.

So there were few refrigerators in Shell Lake in 1939. Almost everyone had an icebox in which milk, butter and other perishables were kept. Each house was provided with a sign which showed how large a piece of ice they needed that day. It would show the need for twenty-five, fifty, seventy-five or one hundred pounds, based upon which side of the sign was placed on top when the sign was put in the window. Housewives were uncanny in their ability to estimate how much was needed. However, absolute precision was not required because the chunk could be reduced and shaped with an ice pick, a gadget resembling a screwdriver, but with a very sharp point.

Each day I worked at this, the routine was as follows: Dode and I showed up at the icehouse at 7:30 A.M. We shoveled and swept the sawdust from four chunks and with an ice-saw, divided each of them into fourths. We would then load the sixteen chunks on an old Reo Speed-Wagon flatbed truck. Next, we would travel a predetermined route until we saw a sign in a window. In response to the size ordered, we sawed that amount from the larger chunk, grabbed it with ice tongs and carried it into the house to place in the icebox. We did not handle any money, because the customer paid the bill at the icehouse. This arrangement may have been instigated out of concern that Dode might siphon off a portion of the proceeds to acquire liquor. I'm not sure.

At this juncture I want to say that Dode was never a problem during those two weeks. He always had a bottle of whiskey with him, and every now and then would take a snort. But it never seemed to affect his performance. He always arrived at work on time. He was a hard worker and I very much enjoyed assisting him. And once or twice a day he would let me drive the old Reo truck, which had a lever that engaged the "high speed rear end". That was a feature I never used, never really understood, and never again ran across during my entire life.

One more thing: the kids loved to see us come with the ice. We always had a generous supply of ice chips for them, providing a free cold treat on a hot summer day.

CHAPTER 19
AT THE UNIVERSITY OF WISCONSIN

At age sixteen, I graduated from Brooklyn High School. Shortly afterwards they tore it down and bussed the kids to Oregon. Some clarification may be required. It was Brooklyn, Wisconsin and not New York. Further, it was Oregon, Wisconsin and not the beautiful State of Oregon where I now live.

There were a variety of jobs that helped me get through the University of Wisconsin in Madison. Or more realistically stated, that carried me through a turbulent, albeit interesting first year at that august institution.

The list comprises waiting on tables in a cooperative student residence, washing test tubes in a biology lab, working in a foundry, typing medical information, working as an orderly at the university hospital, and dehydrating milk and eggs at Bowman Dairy in Brooklyn, which is only sixteen miles from Madison. A long chapter could be written about each of these, but I will refrain, and simply give you a paragraph or two about some of them. A number of them were performed concurrently and all but two were part-time jobs.

One of the full-time jobs was working in an iron foundry. I performed that one for forty hours a week or more for the entire summer between my first year at the University, and my reporting to the service of Uncle Sam. The foundry work was demanding and dirty. But whether it was knocking slag off of a casting or watching a pour of molten metal, it was an enjoyable challenge. I had to struggle with the title of "The College Kid", which was bestowed upon me by the crusty old timers. But they ultimately adopted me as one of their own. It was my first introduction to a labor union, which I had to join. This gave me insight and understanding as to its organization and operation. The knowledge was to come in handy later in life when I would be closely involved with both labor and management. I recall that I always went home from work very dirty and dead-tired.

The other full-time job was that of being an orderly in the university hospital. That involved many things, including the administration of enemas and the manipulation and subsequent cleaning of bedpans. At times it was a trifle messy. But it was almost always interesting. Most of the orderlies were pre-med students and the doctors assumed I also was. I never denied it. So they would occasionally call me over to the bed where they were working. This was so that they could show me something extraordinary. It was often some unique condition, such as an especially ugly bedsore.

I attended a couple of post mortems, where the cadaver is sliced open and completely examined. It included the removing, measuring and weighing of the internal organs. I advise you to skip any such opportunity you may be offered, unless you enjoy hearing women scream and seeing men vomit! I am proud to report that I made it through both of them without mishap.

Because I was a "gofer" for solutions and other supplies, my duties occasionally brought me to the operating room area. The surgical nurses loved to embarrass the young kid and watch him blush. The language in an operating room can get descriptive, and at times raw.

My time was split between the psychiatric ward and men's surgery and urology. In the latter service, one of our tasks was to care for the recently deceased. We had to fill out and attach the toe tag. We had to stuff all orifices with cotton, cover the cadaver with a sheet, and wheel the gurney to a far off location on the top floor of the hospital. It was there at the morgue that we had to roll the body onto a shelf, and slide the shelf back into the refrigerator. This was a particularly scary task in the late night and early morning hours because the elevator was old and creaky and one could hear dogs barking and baying. The dogs were being used in medical experiments.

There was one orderly who was both nerdy and opinionated, and therefore thoroughly disliked by everyone. In response to this problem, one of my contemporaries hatched a nefarious plot. I was innocent, as it was not my shift that particular night. When the unpopular fellow arrived for duty at midnight, he was told that "a stiff" was all prepared for the morgue and he was to do the delivery. Another orderly, who was very much alive, was under the sheet. When the very scariest part of the journey was nearing its end, the stiff sat up under the sheet. The terrified orderly took off at high speed and we were told that he never even came back to pick up his pay.

The other half of my hospital work was performed at Bradley Memorial, the psychiatric ward. It was there that I became absolutely fascinated by that remarkable instrument we call the brain. I was not supposed to read the charts. But late at night, after completion of the major work, such as caring for the patients and getting them to bed, what else was there to do? Study? Surely you jest. Study at this stage of my life was simply out of the question!

I did not understand much of what I read in the charts, but the portions that I did understand simply blew me away. I'm sure psychiatrists have learned a lot in the ensuing sixty-five years, but my guess is that they still haven't even scratched the surface. Two personal experiences may shed some light on why the human mind is such a mystery for me.

One middle-aged male patient was a particular favorite of mine. He was congenial, seemingly happy and well adjusted. Whenever time allowed, he and I would discuss literature, politics, philosophy and many other subjects. I often wondered why he was there. That is until one night when he attempted to do me in. He had somehow acquired a table knife. He came up behind me babbling unintelligible things and screaming that he was going to kill me. I was terrified and ran from him while screaming at least as loud as he. An alert orderly quickly arrived on the scene and distracted his attention just long enough so that the two of us could get him down. A nurse appeared immediately and administered a calming shot. To him, not me! It was an ugly experience, but the next day we resumed our scholarly discussions as if nothing unusual had happened between us.

Another male patient reminded me of a wild animal. He constantly raved and cursed, and for months was confined by leather restraints on all four limbs. Before the end of my work at the hospital, I saw this man cured and released. I carried his suitcase down to his family's car and we exchanged jovial goodbyes.

Who can really explain these two extremes? And what accounts for the fact that some savants can memorize a phonebook or instantly tell you the number of individual items there are in a huge, conglomerate array?

Others can tell you what day of the week it was on any date you name from many years ago. What marvelous discoveries lie ahead of us as we continue to study what goes on inside the human brain? Maybe I should have pursued a career in psychiatry, but it always sort of scared me after I learned that every psychiatrist has a psychiatrist!

My most lucrative job during my first year at the University came from a doctor. He had placed an ad with the student employment center. I responded to the ad, he interviewed me, and hired me a couple of days later. The job was to type information on three by five inch cards. He had underlined the information in articles that he had removed from medical journals. He paid me fifty cents per card, which I think he believed to be fair because of the difficulty of the text. Typing was the best course I ever had in high school. Sixty-five words a minute, with no errors, was my cup of tea. I caught onto the medical language rather quickly and hence was able to crank out an average of four cards an hour. Can you imagine earning the huge sum of two dollars an hour, in a thirty-five cents an hour world? I think his wife figured it out. She took over the job herself after a couple of months.

At one point, I arranged my classes so that I could hitchhike the sixteen miles from Madison to Brooklyn. That allowed me to work three nights each week on the "graveyard shift" at Bowman Dairy. So on each of those nights I went to work at midnight and worked until eight a.m. I never did get used to those crazy hours. My stomach was upset during the entire period.

They had a much better equipped factory than had been the case at the creamery in Shell Lake. An added feature was that they also dehydrated eggs. The process was different. The thoroughly mixed, liquid eggs were sprayed in a very fine mist from the ceiling of a large and extremely hot room. By the time the spray had fallen to the bottom of the room, it had changed into a powder.

The barrel routine, with weighing, filling and stenciling was the same as for milk, which I have already described in detail. Our boss, Nick Christiansen was a good supervisor and reflected considerably more couth than did my former creamery supervisor, Gib Linton. This job provided me another experience with a labor union.

Shortly after I left this employment, the factory was torn down. It was replaced with housing units. That's two factories and a high school that have met this horrible fate soon after meeting me. Maybe I should take it personally!

Chapter 20
SERVICE TO MY COUNTRY

During my first year at college, I did not establish any notable scholastic records. When the year ended I had attained a 0.1 grade point average. This is not to be confused with a 1.0 GPA! Furthermore, I was placed on final probation for a variety of reasons. I considered each one of them to be valid. But remember, World War II was in progress. There were many who shared my philosophy at that particular time: "Eat, drink and be merry, for tomorrow you may die"!

I tried to join the Navy's programs of V5 and V12. Neither program would have me. The latter had no vacancies and the former would not accept me. They thought that my slight overbite was a problem. After flying a fighter plane for a couple of hours, they believed that I would become fatigued from biting down on the mouthpiece of an oxygen mask.

My brother Royce had been accepted into the United States Merchant Marine Academy at Kings Point, New York. I applied, but was turned down because of my being overweight. But they promised me that they would try to get me in on a waiver. And so it was that I remained at home for a while, specializing in dating girls. At that particular time in our history, the odds were incredibly good, because so many young men were in the armed forces.

Meanwhile, my number came up in the draft. Accordingly, I was treated to a very uncomfortable ride on a school bus, from Shell Lake to Milwaukee. This is a distance of about 350 miles. The purpose of the journey was to get a pre-induction physical exam. They had no problem with my overbite or weight. I passed with flying colors. My success was probably due to the fact that my body was warm to the touch! When they asked which branch I preferred, I chose the Marine Corps without hesitation.

When I returned to Shell Lake, I advised Oran Plahn, the chairman of our Draft Board, that I had been accepted for the Marine Corps. However, I reminded him of the possible waiver to attend Kings Point. "What about that?" I asked. There was a twenty-one day wait between the physical exam and actual induction. So chairman Plahn said to me: "If the waiver arrives in the mail in the next three weeks, you will go to the Academy. If not, welcome to the Marine Corps".

The three-week period was to end on a Monday. On the previous Friday, I received the waiver in the mail. So instead of fighting hand-to-hand combat in such places as Saipan or Tinian, I was selected for Kings Point. You may be thinking that this was a safer choice. Few people know that the United States Merchant Marine Academy had more deaths per capita during WWII than did the United States Marine Corps. The reason is that so many ships were sunk. There were usually two Kings Pointers on each ship.

I went to basic training for four and a half months at Coyote Point in San Mateo, California. A classmate and I then boarded a merchant vessel, the El Salvador Victory. The ship was to operate in the Pacific carrying men and supplies. We were at Okinawa the day the war ended. After the War, in 1946 at age twenty, I returned to Kings Point to complete a first class education. In addition, I earned sixty-five dollars a month plus room, board, and medical coverage. Needless to say, I was unable to add much to my savings account during this period of time. Before we were sworn into the Maritime Service, we were sworn into the Naval Reserve. So I was called to active duty by the navy during the Korean Conflict, and reported aboard a destroyer. It was the USS Hank (DD702), which at the time was anchored in Guantanamo Bay, Cuba. I then held the rank of Lieutenant Junior Grade and spent a year on this vessel. Since it had just come back from a tough tour of duty in Korea, it was rewarded with a goodwill cruise to Europe. The ports-of-call were to include Londonderry in Ireland, Portsmouth and Bristol in England, Marseille, Paris and Rouen in France, Ostend Belgium, Bremerhaven Germany and Alicante, Spain.

Just prior to our goodwill cruise, we were ordered to the Davis Strait, located between Greenland and Baffin Island. That operation was for the purpose of conducting anti-submarine warfare exercises. Accompanying us were one aircraft carrier and one submarine. Several days into the exercises, our captain assigned me to be an observer for seventy-two hours. That assignment provided me with three of the most memorable and exciting days of my life.

On day one, I was transferred by breeches buoy from the destroyer to the aircraft carrier. This part of the Atlantic Ocean can be rather wild and the seas were running high. When the two ships heeled toward each other, I dropped down almost into the water. During the next few moments, the two ships heeled away from each other and I was flung skyward like a rocket. It was truly more exciting and scary than any concession ride imaginable. And I did not even have to pay for a ticket!

After what seemed like a wild hour or two, but probably only fifteen or twenty minutes, I arrived safely on the deck of the aircraft carrier and was given a tour of the premises. That was followed by a wonderful lunch. Carrier food is superior to destroyer food by a very wide margin. It included ice cream, which at that time could not be produced on a destroyer. Being a Wisconsin boy, it is only natural that dairy products such as "gedunk" are near and dear to my heart. Why sailors called ice cream by that name is anybodies guess!

Shortly after lunch, I was treated to a plane ride in one of the heaviest single engine (conventional, not jet) planes the navy had. By the time we cleared the end of the catapult, we were pinned to the back of our seats by an unbelievable G-Force. Worse than that, we were losing altitude and were lower than the carrier deck and just barely above the sea. Believe me, I was holding my breath until the powerful engine won the battle and we started to climb.

I was in the electronic technician's seat, well behind the pilot. There was only a tiny porthole, which provided me with a very limited view of the outside world. Shortly after takeoff, the pilot called me on the radio to check on my welfare and to advise me that he had some bad news. He said: "I can't get the wheels up". Cheerfully, I responded: " it would be worse news if you couldn't get the wheels down!" He liked my positive attitude. But he had some more bad news. "The radio connection to the carrier has failed". I was unable to come up with a suitable quip for that announcement. But he put me at ease when he added: "It is routine for me to notify the ship by flying directly over it, waggling the wings and then coming around for a landing".

This sounded easy enough until the pilot actually did it. I was peering out the porthole at the tiny spot on the ocean that bobbed like a cork and realized that it was to be our "landing field". The deck heaved up and down as well as back and forth. We landed at a speed of one hundred and twenty knots (137 miles per hour) and in a few feet were at zero miles per hour. Let me just say that the breeches buoy experience seemed like small potatoes in comparison. However, it was over and we were safe. I think the six-minute duration of the flight set some sort of record for brevity. We should have submitted it for inclusion in the Guinness Book of Records!

My final assigned duty on the aircraft carrier was to stand behind the Carrier Landing Officer, at the extreme aft port corner of the flight deck. He's the person you see in the old war movies, who holds the two paddles and signals the incoming pilot that he is too high or two low, too fast or too slow. He also signals him to either cut his engines or accept a wave-off, requiring him to circle the carrier and try again. Interestingly, this is all done these days with a system of colored lights instead of a person holding paddles. But back then, it was really scary standing behind him and seeing the planes come whizzing by just a few feet away. I certainly learned what we had looked like when we landed earlier in the day. Standing on deck, I was told that if anything went wrong, I was simply to jump into the net. That net hung over the side of the ship, about ten to twenty feet below the deck level. It looked very small to me. If you missed it, you were destined to fall a long way into the sea. Fortunately, all went well and I did not have to jump.

My carrier observation duties had now been completed and my next assignment was to be on a submarine. I was flown by helicopter to the surfaced submarine, where I was lowered to the deck on a cable. Prior to landing on the deck, I was unintentionally smashed against the conning tower several times. It was very painful, but luckily none of my body parts were damaged. Remember, the sea was rough and a surfaced sub is not the most stable platform for which one could hope.

When I climbed, first up and then down into the interior of the sub, the captain immediately called out the order "DIVE, DIVE". And dive we did and we stayed down for forty-eight hours. The objective here was to run as deeply and as silently as possible, and to zigzag so that neither the destroyer nor the planes from the carrier could zero in on our location.

I have spent some time in confined spaces in my life, but this was ridiculous. Modern day nuclear subs are roomier, but on that sub it was difficult even to climb into a bunk. And the air got progressively more pungent, until by the end of the second day my eyes burned and I was having difficulty breathing. Besides that, I was trying to stay out of everybody's way. It was not easy. Trying to pass another person in a passageway presented a difficult problem for both of us.

The second day, during lunch in the Officers Mess, I listened to my fellow diners boast about how much smarter the Submarine Corps was than the other branches of the navy. I could not let this go on without defending our sonar operators. These are the men who spend their spare time listening to records of sonar sounds. You probably know about Doppler Effect. If a train is coming toward you with its horn blowing, the pitch of the sound rises. The converse is true once the train passes. This effect is much more subtle with sonar, but lots of practice hones one's skills.

Just then, in the course of our conversation, we heard and felt a loud thud. You can imagine my alarm at any strange sound while deep beneath the surface of the sea. I nervously blurted out: "What in the hell was that?" One of the officers responded somewhat sheepishly, with:

"That was a dummy hedgehog landing on the deck". I won't go into a lengthy explanation of hedgehogs, but will simply say that in the real world of combat, the inhabitants of that sub would no longer have had to sweat the small stuff! It was certainly gratifying for me to have just defended the skills of the sonar operators, and for them to have then so effectively proven my point.

After twenty-four hours, the sub surfaced and a helicopter magically appeared to take me "home". I had all but forgotten the rough sea, because beneath the surface it had been totally calm. I had great difficulty putting the sling around me because of the heaving deck. The whirlybird folks were then able to reel in the line and after a couple more bangs against the conning tower, raised me up into the helicopter. A few minutes later they lowered me onto the deck of the destroyer.

During the "crash course" on anti-submarine warfare, I'd been bumped, bruised, hoisted, flung, and scared out of my wits. More importantly, I had the immense thrill of having been on an aircraft carrier, catapulted in a navy plane, on a helicopter, and submerged in a submarine, all for the first time. I'd had three wonderfully exciting and never-to-be-forgotten days.

Destroyer life was less than pleasant because of the over-crowding and the way the ship tossed about in rough weather. I never enjoyed bad weather at sea, but at the end of WWII my ship had survived Typhoon Louise, one of the most devastating storms the Pacific has ever seen. I had somehow overcome that challenge so I planned to just tough it out on the Hank.

Every officer on the ship except me had applied for a transfer. In true government fashion, I was the only officer to receive an order to transfer.

It arrived while the ship was in Bristol, England so I was able to enjoy nearly all of the "Goodwill Cruise".

Because of his photographic experience, my brother had tried several times to get his Service Specialty Designator changed, from Line Officer to Photography Specialist. Alas, it never happened for him. But as for me, I was ordered off the Hank and assigned to the Naval Photographic Center in Anacostia, Maryland for a year. Go figure!

The job was to produce and direct Navy Training films. I loved it! It gave me an opportunity to work with some very skilled people. A particularly good friend from whom I learned a great deal was Rudy Nelson, who had been the Assistant Special Effects Director at Paramount Studios. Some years later we would visit the Nelson family in Hollywood. During that visit, I was able to spend a good deal of time on the set for the filming of "The Ten Commandments". On several occasions I was lucky enough to rub elbows with Charleton Heston and Yvonne DeCarlo, who starred in the film.

The navy admiral in charge of shipboard living-conditions requested a film that would help him with his task to make improvements. Our skipper assigned it to me, since I had just recently been at sea. After a short consultation with the admiral, I set out to write, produce and direct a grim but truthful portrayal of how bad the living conditions at sea really were.

One morning, the skipper announced: "I am leaving on a trip, but would like to review your film before I leave". Since it was nearly "in the can" (movie-speak for finished), I set up a personal screening for him the next day. Following the protocol for the situation, I sat behind the Old Man (skipper) at the screening. As the film progressed, I was sure I could see his ears getting redder and redder.

At the conclusion, the house lights came up. The skipper arose from his seat, turned to face me, and said: "The admiral better like it". He then strode quickly out of the room. I had the sudden feeling that my naval career was in jeopardy and perhaps even hanging in the balance. I spent a couple of somewhat restless nights wondering and worrying about it. But when the admiral saw the film several days later, it turned out to be exactly what he wanted and he loved it. Shipboard living conditions started to improve almost immediately. Although the admiral deserves most of the credit, there are many thousands of sailors who never knew how I jeopardized my career in order to help them be a bit more comfortable.

Another great advantage of being in Anacostia was that it was right next to Washington, D.C. It was such a pleasure to be able to have my wife and son with me full-time. That was a nice contrast to the infrequent visits I had while stationed on a ship. During the year we lived there, we had numerous opportunities to spend an entire day at well-known places in and around the city. Typically, tourists might have only twenty minutes or so at any one of these. Our son, John got to roll Easter eggs on the White House lawn at age three. Dwight D. Eisenhower was our President at that time.

We lived in the same apartment building as a Secret Service agent who guarded President Eisenhower. How fortunate it was for us that he was able to show us parts of the White House that tourists never see. His name is Doug Duncan and he became a very close friend. Sadly his wife Mary became the first polio victim in Washington during that year. Doug and Mary decided to send their three children to live for a short time with grandparents in California. We volunteered to take one of them, baby Eddie, into our home until his mother recovered to the point where she could again take care of him. They agreed and the arrangement worked out well. Recently, I believe it was in 2001, we had the pleasure of spending an entire day with the wonderful Duncan family, who now reside in California.

So with a total of five years on active duty and twenty years in the naval reserve, I retired. As my brother once said: "I wouldn't trade my experiences for a million dollars, but I would not want to go through it again for a million dollars". Amen to that! I still recall that on one of his two trips to Murmansk, they lost half of the ships in the convoy. Thank you, brother, for your contribution to the safety of our country.

During my time on active duty in the navy, I earned in excess of two hundred dollars a month, plus room and board for me and medical coverage for my family. But by this time I had a wife and young son to support, so after paying for their room and board I had little or nothing left for the savings account.

I almost blush when people ask me if I am a veteran of the fracas which is sometimes referred to as the "Korean Conflict". My ship, the Hank certainly was, but she left the "the action" just before I was ordered aboard. Accordingly, I never got within ten thousand miles of Korea during the entire time and the possibility of my perishing never even entered my mind. But I am an official member of the veteran group and therefore received G.I. Bill assistance to finish college and purchase a new house.

On the other hand, I am extremely proud to have been granted official status as a veteran of World War II, where I did face death on several occasions. To this date, I am sorry to report that the Merchant Mariners, whose loss of life ratio was extremely high, have never received anything in the way of GI benefits. President Franklin D. Roosevelt publicly stated that he hoped they would be recognized as veterans. That was not to happen until many years later. They were granted the name but no benefits whatsoever.

A bill is now in congress to correct the inequity, but its passage remains doubtful at this time. The House of Representatives passed it with a significant majority, but Senator Akaka, the chairman of the Veterans' Affairs Committee, will not release the companion bill from his committee for a vote on the floor of the Senate. This is true in spite of the fact that sixty-two senators are signed on as co-sponsors. Ah well, nobody ever claimed that democracy was perfect!

CHAPTER 21
SHOES AND PHOTOGRAPHY

In late 1947, after graduating from the United States Merchant Marine Academy at Kings Point, I returned to Monroe, Wisconsin, the city of my birth. There I entered into a partnership with my brother, Royce, in the operation of a photography studio. It was appropriately named "ZumBrunnen Studio".

During my spare time at the academy, I had acquired some skill in color-tinting photographs. This was done with oil-based paints and a variety of the same brushes used by artists. The technique was very popular before the advent of color-photography. I will never forget the first two pictures Royce gave me to color. One was of a bride who had dozens and dozens of tiny flowers in her bouquet. The other was of a child who obviously had Down Syndrome. The photo clearly reflected several spots of drool. Happily, at the end of these two very arduous tasks, we had a happy bride and a happy mother.

My brother had almost all of the creative and artistic talent. My contribution was to hold up the chemistry end. I regularly labored for long hours in the darkroom. We shared covering candid wedding shoots and the action stuff. That included things like ball games and the county fair activities. In thinking back, I suppose we greatly complemented each other's skills. Unfortunately, we both thought we were contributing the greater effort and value to the business.

It had also become apparent that the business could not support two families. I had recently married Ruth Ann Ellefson. She was born and raised in Monroe, and worked at the Swiss Colony, a purveyor of cheese. So I sold my interest in the enterprise to Royce and he continued the operation for several years. It is probably appropriate to admit that neither one of us made a fortune from photography.

A week or so after leaving ZumBrunnen Studio, a friend told me that Henry Kundert was looking for someone to work with him in his shoe store. I applied and after a short interview he hired me. Henry was the best boss I ever had. He taught me the retail shoe business, and a great deal more about the really important values in life. He was honest, patient, and understanding. I hope some of his wonderful virtues rubbed off on me and have been guiding me through life.

Perhaps an incident or two from my short career in shoe sales might illustrate the point. One day a farmer came into the store, wearing a pair of work shoes I had sold him the previous week. His complaint was that: "These shoes smell funny and I think I am entitled to a new pair." I examined the shoes and had to partially agree with him. But the smell I detected was clearly that of barnyard manure. I considered myself something of an expert on that particular subject, having had rather extensive experience on a farm.

The customer acknowledged that they did indeed smell of manure but also of something else. Henry had overheard the conversation and came over to say hello to the man. "Give him a new pair", he said. The customer was happy and after he left, Henry said to me: "I firmly believe in the old saying about the customer always being right". He pointed out that this had cost him a few dollars, but that we had a happy customer who would more than likely be buying shoes from the Kundert Shoe Store for the rest of his life.

On another day, a lady came in and wanted a new pair of dress shoes. I tried more than twenty pairs on her but in the end, she walked out without purchasing a pair. I was quite irate, facing the task of re-boxing all of the shoes and putting them back in stock, without having made a sale. Henry could see that I was upset. He approached me with a smile and said simply: "Dont let it get you down. Your pay is the same whether or not you made the sale". His pleasant words immediately calmed me down.

I am certain that had I remained at his store he would have taken me on as a partner. But my desire to return to the University of Wisconsin was a strong one. I knew Henry was very fond of me and had enjoyed our working relationship as much as I had. But I admired the man even more when I announced my plan. He immediately recognized that it had been very difficult for me to tell him I was leaving. He expressed joy in my decision and said that he believed it to be an intelligent move. He then told me: "Young man, you have been an excellent employee. You will be greatly missed around here. But I have very high hopes for your future." I believe this was the same response he would have given his own son, if he had been in my position. I certainly appreciated his words and was strongly encouraged by them. Henry will forever remain in my memory as one of the finest men I ever knew.

Chapter 22

BACK TO COLLEGE

When I requested permission to return to the University of Wisconsin at Madison, they reminded me that I was still on final probation. I told them I had graduated from Kings Point with honors, but that the academy was not yet accredited. They advised me that they would review my case and would "get back to me". That advice reminded me somewhat of the Hollywood phrase "Don't call us, we'll call you", which roughly translated usually means "Don't hold your breath!"

Miraculously, the following week I received notification that the academy had been accredited and that I now held a Bachelor's Degree in Marine Transportation. I immediately phoned the people at the University of Wisconsin and told them I would like to register for the semester which was to start in a couple of weeks. They reminded me: "We are still evaluating your previous request." I replied: "I wish to cancel the previous request and apply for entry into graduate school." I think they found this somewhat amusing. None-the-less, they called back a couple of days later with their decision.

"We want you to register for the upcoming semester as a Special Senior

Student". "But that isn't grad school" I replied plaintively. Their response made sense. "Grad school limits you to 12 units per semester. At that rate, it would take you a long time to get a master's degree, especially having to start with Accounting 101A. But a Special Senior Student can take as many units as practicable."

Actually, I was delighted to be readmitted under any circumstances. For the next two years I averaged about nineteen units per semester, with a top of twenty-one. That particular semester I had six final exams, three of them in one day. My earnings during this period were limited to some small side jobs, but Ruth Ann worked at the University Book Store full time, and I also worked there during the rush periods.

A year prior to receiving my MBA, the Korean Conflict broke out, and the Navy advised me that they desperately needed my presence. That delayed my life plans for two years. But subsequent to that hiatus, I immediately returned to school and received help from the GI Bill. Working as a graduate teaching assistant was also of value. We had enough income that my wife did not need to work and could devote all of her time and effort to our son John, who had by then arrived on the scene.

During the time between my return to the University and my graduation, I earned twenty-two A's and two B's in the twenty-four classes I took. That convinced the admissions department that they had made a good decision. Furthermore, I was not summoned to the Dean's Office even once during that entire period. But did I graduate with honors of any kind? The answer is an emphatic "No!" But how can that be true? It was, of course, because of my freshman year grade point average of 0.1. And once again, I feel obliged to remind the reader not to confuse that with a 1.0!

And as Dean Elwell handed me my sheepskin on a very hot June afternoon at Camp Randall Stadium, his words still ring in my ears. He said: "Congratulations ZumBrunnen! At last you are off of final probation!" He was correct. There were only two ways to accomplish this. You either had to graduate or die. Fortunately, I had accomplished the former!

CHAPTER 23

THE CAREER

At the time of my graduation from college, there were eight very large firms of certified public accountants. They were known as the "Big Eight". My wife and I had decided that we would like to live in the San Francisco Bay Area. I had spent a good deal of time there during WWII and had impressed her with stories of shirt sleeve weather on New Years Day, sunshine on almost every day of the year, and the paucity of snow shovels.

I selected three of these large firms and signed up for interviews on campus. I informed each of them that I wanted to be in their San Francisco office. All three made an offer. I selected Ernst & Ernst for several reasons, including the obvious quality of the managing partner of the office. He flew from San Francisco to Madison to take us out to dinner. That included my friend and classmate Dick Nelson and our wives. He invited both Dick and me to join his office. We accepted the offer and were never sorry about our choice. For the next thirty years they treated us extremely well and presented us with many opportunities. Along the way, we were both admitted to partnership.

The partner who had made such a favorable impression on us was Warren Reid. He offered me a starting salary of three hundred twenty-five dollars a month. That was about what the navy had paid me a year before, except the navy had thrown in my room and board. However, this career job was more fun. I passed the rigorous exam to become a certified public accountant and the rest, as they say, is history.

Early in my career, they asked me to open an office for them in San Jose. That city was in the heart of what was to become known as Silicon Valley. This was not only a fine opportunity, but proved to be a challenging one on many occasions that were to follow.

I'm sure that you have a picture in your mind of what a CPA looks like. I was well aware of that image and promised myself that if two people in a row ever guessed that I was a CPA, I would immediately change careers. More often than not, people guessed that I was a salesman. In reality, I suppose that's what I have always been. Selling someone on you and on your abilities and ideas is not always easy, but it is certainly an important factor in developing a successful career.

People are shocked when I tell them that I hate detail. I really do. I always rose to the occasion on the many times I needed to work with details, but I always preferred what is commonly referred to as the "big picture". For example, there was nothing I liked better than to walk through the factory of a newly acquired client, and to quickly notice the many areas where improvements could be made.

I think the experienced CPA is to business what the General Practitioner is to medicine. The Physician deals with a myriad of diseases and is expected to recommend techniques to improve the health of the patient. The CPA deals with a large assortment of management philosophies. He or she also comes into contact with all kinds of engineering, production, marketing and finance techniques, and is expected to recommend ways to improve the health of a business. Further, the CPA has total access to the "books", which reflect the productivity, or lack thereof, of all of those combined forces. This places the CPA in a very special position to judge how well things are working—or NOT!

Some of the proudest moments in my career, were the several times I was introduced by one executive to another as "This is the person who saved our company's life". If that doesn't satisfy a person's desire to help people solve problems, I don't know what would.

My entire thirty-year professional career was spent at Ernst and Ernst, which through a merger with a large European firm became Ernst & Whinney. Later, through a subsequent merger with another member of the Big Eight, Arthur Young & Company, it became Ernst & Young. As previously stated, I started at three hundred and twenty five dollars a month. In 1984, the year of my retirement at the age of fifty-eight, I was doing fine, and had managed to stay well ahead of the costs of inflation during the preceding thirty years. Not bad for a former kid salesman of asparagus, pigeons, and horseradish!

Chapter 24
FUN AND GAMES

Before my story ends, I would like to confess that all of my income has not come from jobs, or ideas to sell goods and services. For example, when I was nine years old, I was the second best marbles player in Brooklyn. Only Johnny Paynter was better. I was a shrewd trader of marbles, whether they were shooters, aggies (agates) or peewees, the names given to the various types. These endeavors would sometimes make a little profit for me. How fortunate I was that no peddlers' license was required to sell marbles. Nor were any of my activities ever to come under the scrutiny of the Securities and Exchange Commission!

From around the age of ten, I was a frequent visitor to our local pool emporium. The proprietor charged us a "nickel a cue", which when translated into laymen's terms means five cents per person, per game. We would place very small bets on the outcome. The size of the bet was just enough so that the winner would get his nickel back, plus a modest profit. I loved shooting pool. From a competitive standpoint, my ability with a pool cue could probably be best described as slightly above average.

Please do not think I was a "hustler" ala Minnesota Fats, or Paul Newman's character in the movie entitled "The Hustler". I never shot pool with strangers, so my opponents always knew what they were up against. Having already quantified my performance level, adjectives such as "formidable and awesome" might sound a bit excessive. But being somewhat of a competitive animal, I was generally a force with which to be reckoned. I have never denied my competitive spirit and suspect that it became a part of my character development rather early in life.

Playing poker in college and while in the merchant marine and navy produced a small net gain. I also loved to play bridge and enjoyed playing for modest amounts, such as a tenth or twentieth of a cent per point of score differential.

The game of dominoes was played just for fun as a child, but during my adult working career it was frequently the game of choice while relaxing after work. A typical wager was two dollars a game plus twenty cents a point of difference in the score. That was doubled for "skunks", the name given to the situation where you or your team were less than half way around the board at the end of the game. I played with some real "sharks", and though I didn't keep an account of the results I was probably fortunate to come somewhere near breaking even.

In spite of it being technically illegal, I would hazard a guess that perhaps you might have occasionally placed a bet or two on a golf game. If players' handicaps were always honest, and that's a big "if", such bets should pretty well break even over the long haul. That is more than likely about how it worked out for me. I was a decent golfer and was always honest regarding my handicap. My lowest handicap was thirteen, and I have had only one "hole-in-one" so far. But at my advanced age, and now requiring a cane or a walker, I am dreaming of a grand comeback this year or next!

You may be dubious, hearing me tell you that I think I made a little money at various racetracks over the years. Those who do the best are the ones who rise early on race days and go to the track to watch the morning workouts. Horses are similar to people in some regards. For example, there are days when we are just not feeling one hundred percent. Accordingly, we are not willing, or even able to do our best. That covers just about everything and surely includes running a race. The experienced attendee at the early morning workouts is sometimes able to recognize the problem.

Going to the morning workouts never did appeal to me, but I had some wonderful tutoring from Ron Casriel, a close friend of mine at work. Ron had studied the ponies from early childhood, and over the years had learned a lot. He taught me how to study the horses' prior performances under varying track conditions. He told me to look for hints of trouble in the paddock, when the horses are being displayed and the jockeys are mounting their steeds. It's a very inexact "science", but it sure beats placing your bets on hunches. My advice to you is to never bet on a horse because of its color or size or the fact that the jockey has blue eyes. Betting based upon that kind of stuff could become somewhat costly over time!

In the casinos, my goal has always been to minimize my losses. It doesn't take a brain surgeon to figure out that the owners of casinos are making a profit. In the name of entertainment, I have sometimes spent a few dollars on shooting craps, playing roulette, or on the slot machines. But the most favorable odds are with the playing of blackjack which is frequently known by the name "twenty-one". I am what is known as a card counter. That would really bore most people because it requires a lot of concentration. However, the investment in time can be quite beneficial. I always limited the amount I was willing to lose and never tried to win it back on that occasion. As a result, I frequently lost my designated amount. But there were times that I was able to walk away with a modest gain. Had I spent as much effort in tracking wins and losses as was spent in counting cards, I'm almost certain that the records would reflect a modest loss over the years. To me, that begs an answer to the age-old question: "If one sets out to lose, and then does so, has he or she been successful?"

A friend of mine, Tony Starbird introduced me to a fabulous dice game called Double Chooseys. It is rather complex and actually involves a great number of games including Liars' Dice. When it is your turn to select any one of the many qualifying games, your opponent has the option of refusing your first offer. But the refusal results in the obligation to play your second offered game. I think you can imagine the chicanery involved in being a good Double Chooseys player. I proved to be a pretty competent participant in this challenging arena and was able to cover the cost of a portion of numerous luncheons. That was in addition to pocketing a little cash. In summary, doesn't one have to conclude that chicanery and the ability to lie are not always bad things?

These "money making?" endeavors were all fun and I have no regrets for having participated. They have each contributed to the pleasure, recreation and knowledge in my life. So perhaps a "worst case result" evaluation is that I was able to enjoy many gratifying, free-time hours at minimal cost. In the aggregate, I might have come out a little ahead. But come to think about it, isn't that what any gambler will tell you?

Two other more serious involvements need mentioning because of their overall importance to my financial well-being. The first of these is real estate. I sold approximately twenty of my residences through the years.

In most cases, the purchase of each one of them has included all of the net-proceeds received from the sale of their immediate predecessor, plus a bit more. However, the last four in the series generated cash, a pretty respectable amount of it, to add to my nest egg.

The other major contributor to my financial health was the stock market. It was there that I tried to achieve the advice of the multitudes through the ages, which is to "buy low and sell high"! I must admit that this has been pretty much of a "no-brainer" during most of the years that I was able to buy securities. The "bears" chased away the "bulls" on occasion but that condition never lasted very long. Unfortunately, I made a couple of bad picks along the way and had to suffer the consequences. Even so, my holdings increased rather handsomely during my years of buying stocks and bonds.

Those who know me well are of the opinion that I am a tad conservative. That is probably why I got scared out of the market for three short periods when it was on the way up. I just could not imagine that the prices could keep on increasing. The first two times they did continue the upward spiral. So I got back in. To my credit, or maybe we should call it "blind dumb luck" the third time I got out was just before the steep decline into the present reccssion. The financial situation doesn't seem likely to improve very much before 2011 at the earliest.

To accomplish success in "buying low" one usually needs a good deal of courage. For example, several months ago I believed the bad economic times were close to bottoming out. Accordingly, I acquired long positions in five "solid" companies with long histories of paying good dividends. Alas, they proceeded to lose about half of their market value over the next two months. Happily, as of this writing three of them are close to what I paid for them, one has fully recovered and I am slightly ahead on the fifth stock.

So just yesterday, I placed a "buy order" for five more stocks that are representative of old established companies with good dividend records. This was an action somewhat contrary to the pervading doom and gloom that most people are expressing about the current economic situation.

Today, two of the five are "up". Dare I think that I was successful in "buying low"? I can only hope. Meanwhile, the market news was rather dismal both yesterday and today. But I'm in it for the long haul, so daily fluctuations don't particularly excite me. After all, is a company intrinsically worth much more or less than it was yesterday, just because the chairman of the Federal Reserve Board made an optimistic or pessimistic comment? I don't think so, but time will tell. Stay tuned!

Chapter 25

CONCLUSION

Tom Brokaw called the people in my age group "The Greatest Generation". I like that appellation, but firmly believe that we were also the luckiest.

As for me, I had the very good fortune early on to learn self-reliance, perseverance, thrift, and optimism. I survived World War II and the Korean conflict. I got a splendid education in the small town school of Brooklyn, Wisconsin. That was followed by graduation from two excellent institutions of higher learning, the United States Merchant Marine Academy and the University of Wisconsin. And then during my career with one of the best accounting firms in the world, the American economy went through one of the longest boom periods in history.

I participated in what was later to be known as organic farming, although we did not recognize it as such. It didn't acquire its name until years later! My life has often been touched by the ideas and practices of "sustainability". I had the opportunity to work in the excitement of the early days of Silicon Valley. The chances presented themselves for me to meet a lot of prominent people, including three Presidents of the United States.

I believe that one of the many important things I learned from life was the importance of returning a meaningful portion of the time, talent and treasure, with which I had been so richly blessed. I have been an officer or board member of dozens of charitable organizations. It was my privilege to be on the Parks and Recreation Commission in San Jose, California and to be a member of the Shell Lake, Wisconsin City Council. I have been a merit badge counselor for the Boy Scouts and have always been a generous financial supporter of many charitable organizations.

As a young boy in rural Wisconsin, I could not have dreamed that these kinds of events and opportunities would come to me. Today, I am comfortably retired and still firmly believe that even if I lost all of my assets, I could still make a living. It would more than likely be a rather modest existence. It is hoped that my point will never have to be proved. But imagination and hard work are a very powerful combination.

On every level, I have had the great good fortune to live the American dream.

Manufactured By: RR Donnelley
                     Momence, IL USA
                     December, 2010